The Digital Marketer's Handbook

Copyright

The Digital Marketer's Handbook
Auteur: Tineke Broeksma
Uitgeverij: RocketRiseMarketing
Vormgeving & DTP: RocketRise Marketing
ISBN: 9798878376808

Table of contents

Chapter 1 - Introduction to Online Marketing

1.1 - History and Evolution: Tracing the growth of online marketing.

The landscape of online marketing has undergone a tremendous transformation since its inception. This evolution mirrors the rapid advancements in technology and the changing behaviors of consumers in the digital age. To appreciate where online marketing stands today, it's crucial to look back at its roots and understand the milestones that have shaped its trajectory.

The Dawn of the Digital Age

The origins of online marketing can be traced back to the early 1990s, coinciding with the public availability of the Internet. This period marked the transition from traditional forms of marketing, which relied heavily on print, radio, and television, to a new era where the digital platform opened up a myriad of possibilities for marketers.

One of the first instances of online marketing was the use of simple websites and email to communicate offers and information to consumers. These tools were rudimentary by today's standards but represented a significant shift in how businesses could reach their audience.

The Advent of Search Engines and SEO

The mid to late 1990s saw the rise of search engines like Yahoo! (1994), Google (1998), and others, which fundamentally changed how information was discovered online. This period marked the birth of Search Engine Optimization (SEO) as marketers realized the importance of ranking higher in search engine results to increase their visibility.

The concept of keywords and the understanding of how search algorithms work became critical components of online marketing strategies. Businesses began to optimize their websites to improve their search rankings, a practice that has since become a cornerstone of digital marketing.

The Social Media Revolution

The early 2000s witnessed the emergence of social media platforms, beginning with sites like MySpace (2003) and LinkedIn (2003), followed by Facebook (2004), Twitter (2006), Instagram (2010), and others. These platforms transformed online marketing by allowing brands to engage directly with their customers in real-time, fostering community and conversation around their products and services.

Social media marketing became a vital strategy for businesses, enabling them to create shareable content, conduct targeted advertising, and gain valuable insights into consumer behavior and preferences.

The Rise of Content and Mobile Marketing

As the Internet became more accessible, particularly with the advent of smartphones and tablets, content marketing and mobile marketing emerged as significant trends. The focus shifted towards creating valuable, relevant, and consistent content to attract and retain a clearly defined audience.

Meanwhile, the proliferation of mobile devices led to the optimization of websites and content for mobile users, recognizing the growing trend of consumers accessing the Internet on the go. This era also saw the introduction of mobile apps and SMS marketing as tools to reach customers more effectively.

The Age of Personalization and Automation

The latest phase in the evolution of online marketing is characterized by personalization and automation. Advances in technology, particularly in artificial intelligence and machine learning, have enabled marketers to offer personalized experiences to their customers based on their preferences, behaviors, and previous interactions.

Marketing automation tools have streamlined various marketing tasks, from email marketing to social media posting and customer relationship management, allowing for more efficient and effective campaigns.

The Future of Online Marketing

Looking ahead, online marketing is set to become even more integrated, immersive, and interactive. Emerging technologies such as augmented reality (AR), virtual reality (VR), and the Internet of Things (IoT) are opening new avenues for creating unique and engaging customer experiences.

The ongoing challenge for marketers will be to stay ahead of the technological curve while maintaining ethical standards and protecting consumer privacy in an increasingly digital world.

Conclusion

The history and evolution of online marketing are a testament to the rapid pace of digital innovation. From the early days of email marketing and simple websites to the complex, data-driven strategies of today, online marketing has become an indispensable part of the business landscape. Understanding its history not only provides context but also offers insights into its future direction, enabling marketers to anticipate trends and adapt their strategies accordingly.

1.2 Key Concepts and Terminology: Understanding the basics.

In the ever-evolving landscape of online marketing, understanding the key concepts and terminology is crucial for anyone looking to navigate this complex field successfully. This chapter aims to demystify the jargon, providing a comprehensive overview of the fundamental terms and concepts that form the backbone of online marketing strategies.

Digital Marketing

Digital Marketing is an umbrella term that encompasses all marketing efforts that use an electronic device or the internet. Businesses leverage digital channels such as search engines, social media, email, and their websites to connect with current and prospective customers. Unlike traditional marketing, which includes print and broadcast, digital marketing allows for two-way communication between businesses and their audience, offering a more personalized and interactive experience.

Search Engine Optimization (SEO)

Search Engine Optimization (SEO) is the practice of increasing the quantity and quality of traffic to your website through organic search engine results. It involves making specific changes to your website design and content that make your site more attractive to a search engine. SEO is often about making small modifications to parts of your website; when viewed individually, these changes might seem like incremental improvements, but when combined with other optimizations, they could have a noticeable impact on your site's user experience and performance in organic search results.

- Keywords: Words or phrases that describe the content on your page or post best. They are the search terms that people enter into search engines.
- Backlinks: Incoming links to a webpage. When a webpage links to any other page, it's called a backlink. In the past, backlinks were the major metric for the ranking of a webpage.
- On-Page SEO: Refers to all measures that can be taken directly within the website in order to improve its position in the search rankings.
- Off-Page SEO: Refers to actions taken outside of your own website to impact your rankings within search engine results pages (SERPs).

Content Marketing

Content Marketing is a strategic marketing approach focused on creating and distributing valuable, relevant, and consistent content to attract and retain a clearly defined audience — and, ultimately, to drive profitable customer action. It's an ongoing process that is best integrated into your overall marketing strategy, and it focuses on owning media, not renting it.

- Content Strategy: The planning, development, and management of content—written or in other media.
- Evergreen Content: Content that is continually relevant and stays "fresh" for readers.

Social Media Marketing (SMM)

Social Media Marketing (SMM) is the use of social media platforms and websites to promote a product or service. Although the terms e-marketing and digital marketing are still dominant in academia, social media marketing is becoming more popular for both practitioners and researchers. Most social media platforms have built-in data analytics tools, enabling companies to track the progress, success, and engagement of ad campaigns.

Pay-Per-Click (PPC)

Pay-Per-Click (PPC) is a model of internet marketing in which advertisers pay a fee each time one of their ads is clicked. Essentially, it's a way of buying visits to your site, rather than attempting to "earn" those visits organically. Search engine advertising is one of the most popular forms of PPC.

Affiliate Marketing

Affiliate Marketing is an online sales tactic that lets a product owner increase sales by allowing others targeting the same audience—"affiliates"—to earn a commission by recommending the product to others. At the same time, it makes it possible for affiliates to earn money on product sales without creating products of their own.

Email Marketing

Email Marketing is a form of direct marketing that uses electronic mail as a means of communicating commercial or fundraising messages to an audience. In its broadest sense, every email sent to a potential or current customer could be considered email marketing.

Conversion Rate Optimization (CRO)

Conversion Rate Optimization (CRO) involves improving the percentage of visitors to a website that convert into customers, or more generally, take any desired action on a webpage. It is commonly referred to in the context of e-commerce, but applies to a variety of contexts including lead generation, subscriptions, and downloads.

Analytics

Analytics in the context of online marketing refers to the measurement, collection, analysis, and reporting of web data for purposes of understanding and optimizing web usage. This can involve the use of tools like Google Analytics, which provides insights into how users find and use a website, helping businesses to improve their marketing strategies.

Understanding these key concepts and terminology is essential for anyone involved in online marketing. This foundational knowledge not only helps in strategizing and implementing effective marketing campaigns but also enables professionals to stay ahead in a rapidly changing digital landscape.

1.3 How Online Marketing Differs from Traditional Marketing: Identifying the unique benefits and challenges.

In the evolving landscape of marketing, the distinction between online and traditional marketing is not just about the medium through which messages are delivered. It's about a fundamental shift in how businesses engage with their audience, measure success, and adapt to consumer behavior. This chapter delves into the core differences between online and traditional marketing, offering insights into why digital strategies have become indispensable in the modern marketing mix.

The Shift from Monologue to Dialogue

Traditional marketing often resembles a monologue, where businesses broadcast messages to a wide audience through channels like television, radio, print ads, and billboards. The communication is one-way, with limited means for the audience to interact directly with the brand. This model places businesses in the role of storytellers who dictate the narrative without real-time feedback.

Online marketing, by contrast, thrives on dialogue. Digital platforms, especially social media, have transformed how businesses communicate, allowing for two-way interactions between brands and consumers. This interactivity fosters a sense of community and engagement, enabling businesses to receive immediate feedback, respond to concerns, and adjust their strategies dynamically. The dialogue nature of online marketing encourages transparency and builds trust, creating deeper relationships with customers.

Targeting Precision and Personalization

One of the most significant advantages of online marketing is its ability to target specific demographics, interests, and behaviors with unprecedented precision. Traditional marketing casts a wide net, hoping to catch the attention of potential customers within a broad audience. This approach can be effective but lacks efficiency, leading to higher costs and lower conversion rates.

Online marketing leverages data analytics and digital tools to segment audiences meticulously, delivering personalized messages that resonate with individual preferences and needs. Search engine optimization (SEO), pay-per-click (PPC) advertising, and social media platforms offer sophisticated targeting options, from geographic location to browsing history. Personalization enhances the consumer experience, increases engagement, and significantly improves the chances of conversion.

Measurability and Data-Driven Decisions

Measuring the effectiveness of traditional marketing campaigns can be challenging. While methods like surveys, focus groups, and sales data provide insights, they often offer a delayed, incomplete picture of a campaign's impact. The lack of real-time data makes it difficult to adjust strategies promptly in response to market changes or campaign performance.

In contrast, online marketing offers comprehensive analytics tools that track a campaign's performance in real time. Digital metrics such as website traffic, click-through rates, social media engagement, and conversion rates offer immediate feedback. This wealth of data enables marketers to make informed decisions, optimize campaigns on the fly, and demonstrate ROI more effectively. The data-driven nature of online marketing supports a culture of continuous improvement and strategic agility.

Cost Efficiency and Scalability

Traditional marketing channels often require significant upfront investment, making them less accessible for small and medium-sized enterprises. The production and placement costs for TV ads, billboards, or print media can be prohibitive, and scaling these efforts involves additional expenditures.

Online marketing, however, offers cost-effective solutions with scalable potential. Digital platforms allow businesses of all sizes to start small and expand their reach as they grow. The flexible pricing models of online advertising, from cost-per-click (CPC) to cost-per-impression (CPM), enable businesses to control their budgets more effectively. Additionally, content marketing and SEO provide long-term value, drawing in customers organically at a fraction of the cost of traditional advertising.

Speed and Adaptability

The pace at which businesses can execute and modify marketing campaigns is another area where online and traditional marketing diverge significantly. Traditional campaigns can take weeks or months to launch, from planning and production to distribution. This slow turnaround time limits a business's ability to respond to market trends or competitor actions quickly.

Online marketing's digital nature allows for rapid deployment and iteration. Social media posts can go live in seconds, email campaigns can be sent in a matter of hours, and ad copy can be adjusted in real time based on performance analytics. This speed and flexibility enable businesses to stay relevant, react to customer feedback, and capitalize on fleeting opportunities in a way that traditional marketing cannot match.

Conclusion

While traditional marketing still holds value, especially in building brand awareness and reaching certain demographics, the advantages of online marketing make it a critical component of any comprehensive marketing strategy. The interactive, targeted, and data-driven nature of digital channels offers unparalleled opportunities for businesses to connect with their audience, optimize their marketing efforts, and achieve measurable results. As technology continues to evolve and consumer behaviors shift increasingly towards digital, the importance of online marketing will only grow, making it essential for businesses to adapt and embrace these digital strategies to succeed in the competitive market landscape.

1.4 Overview of Online Marketing Channels: Exploring SEO, social media, email, content, and PPC.

The digital landscape is vast and varied, offering a plethora of channels through which businesses can reach their target audience. Each channel possesses unique strengths, caters to specific stages of the customer journey, and plays a crucial role in a comprehensive online marketing strategy. This section explores the key online marketing channels: Search Engine Optimization (SEO), Social Media Marketing, Email Marketing, Content Marketing, and Pay-Per-Click (PPC) advertising, providing insights into their importance and how they can be effectively leveraged.

Search Engine Optimization (SEO)

SEO is the art and science of enhancing the visibility of websites and web content in search engine results pages (SERPs). By optimizing for relevant keywords, ensuring website technical health, and creating quality content, businesses can improve their site's ranking, thereby increasing organic (unpaid) traffic. SEO is foundational to online visibility, impacting how easily potential customers can find a business amongst its competitors.

- **Importance**: High rankings in search results are synonymous with increased visibility and credibility in the eyes of consumers. SEO also improves user experience, making it easier for visitors to find the information they need and take action.
- **Strategies**: Effective SEO involves keyword research to understand what potential customers are searching for, on-page optimization (including mobile optimization), off-page strategies like link-building, and technical SEO to ensure the site is search-engine friendly.

Social Media Marketing

Social media platforms like Facebook, Instagram, LinkedIn, and Twitter offer unique opportunities to engage directly with consumers. By creating and sharing content, responding to customer inquiries, and running targeted ads, businesses can build their brand, foster community, and drive traffic to their websites.

- **Importance**: Social media channels offer unparalleled access to large audiences and the ability to engage with them in real-time, fostering a sense of community and loyalty. They also provide valuable data on consumer preferences and behavior.
- **Strategies**: Success in social media marketing requires a consistent posting schedule, high-quality content tailored to each platform, active engagement with followers, and the strategic use of paid advertising options available within these platforms.

Email Marketing

Email marketing involves sending targeted, personalized messages to a segmented list of email subscribers, encouraging them to take action, such as making a purchase or visiting a website. It remains one of the most cost-effective ways to nurture leads and maintain customer loyalty.

- **Importance**: Email marketing allows for direct communication with individuals who have already shown interest in your brand, offering high conversion rates. It's an excellent tool for segmentation and personalization, key factors in modern marketing strategies.
- **Strategies**: Building a healthy email list, segmenting this list based on user behavior or preferences, personalizing messages, and optimizing for mobile devices are crucial strategies. Additionally, A/B testing subject lines and content can significantly improve open and click-through rates.

Content Marketing

Content marketing focuses on creating and distributing valuable, relevant, and consistent content to attract and retain a clearly defined audience. This approach establishes expertise, promotes brand awareness, and keeps your business top of mind for when purchase decisions are made.

- **Importance**: By providing useful content to your audience, you position your brand as a thought leader in your industry. This not only helps with SEO but also builds trust with your audience, making them more likely to choose you over a competitor.
- **Strategies**: Identify your audience's needs and interests and create content that addresses them, whether through blogs, videos, infographics, or podcasts. The content should be promoted across your online channels to maximize reach.

Pay-Per-Click (PPC) Advertising

PPC is a model of internet marketing in which advertisers pay a fee each time one of their ads is clicked. Essentially, it's a way of buying visits to your site, rather than attempting to "earn" those visits organically. Google Ads is one of the most popular PPC platforms.

- **Importance**: PPC can quickly generate traffic and leads and is highly measurable, allowing advertisers to see exactly what they're getting for their investment. It's also highly targeted, enabling advertisers to show their ads to specific demographics, at specific times, and in specific places.
- **Strategies**: Successful PPC campaigns require comprehensive keyword research, the creation of compelling ad copy, the optimization of landing pages, and continuous testing and adjustment to improve performance and ROI.

Each of these channels offers different benefits and serves different purposes within an online marketing strategy. By understanding and leveraging these channels in a way that's cohesive and aligned with their overall marketing goals, businesses can create a powerful online presence that engages and converts their target audience.

1.5 Future of Online Marketing: Predicting upcoming trends.

As we delve into the future of online marketing, it's essential to recognize that the digital landscape is perpetually evolving. Emerging technologies, changing consumer behaviors, and new digital platforms continuously reshape how businesses connect with their audiences. This chapter explores the key trends and predictions that are likely to influence the future of online marketing, offering insights into how marketers can prepare for these changes.

The Rise of Artificial Intelligence and Machine Learning
Artificial Intelligence (AI) and Machine Learning (ML) are set to revolutionize online marketing by enabling more personalized and efficient customer experiences. AI algorithms can analyze vast amounts of data from various sources, including social media, website interactions, and purchase histories, to predict consumer behavior and personalize marketing messages. For example, chatbots and virtual assistants, powered by AI, provide instant customer service and support, enhancing the customer experience and freeing up human resources for more complex tasks.

The Importance of Voice Search Optimization
With the increasing use of digital assistants like Amazon's Alexa, Google Assistant, and Apple's Siri, voice search is becoming an essential part of online marketing strategies. Voice search optimization requires a different approach than traditional text-based SEO. Marketers will need to focus on natural language processing and targeting long-tail keywords that match the conversational tone of voice queries. As voice search grows, ensuring your content is easily discoverable through voice will be crucial.

Augmented Reality (AR) and Virtual Reality (VR) in Marketing

Augmented Reality (AR) and Virtual Reality (VR) offer innovative ways to engage customers by creating immersive experiences. AR allows users to visualize products in their own environment before making a purchase, enhancing the decision-making process. VR, on the other hand, can transport users to virtual settings, offering unique brand experiences. As AR and VR technologies become more accessible, marketers can leverage these tools to create compelling, interactive campaigns.

The Shift Towards Privacy and Data Protection

The future of online marketing will also be shaped by increasing concerns over privacy and data protection. Regulations like the General Data Protection Regulation (GDPR) in Europe and the California Consumer Privacy Act (CCPA) in the United States reflect a growing demand for transparency and control over personal data. Marketers must adapt to these changes by implementing privacy-focused strategies, such as obtaining explicit consent for data collection and offering clear opt-out options. Building trust with consumers through transparent practices will be a key differentiator.

The Emergence of Blockchain Technology

Blockchain technology, best known for its role in cryptocurrencies, offers potential applications in online marketing, particularly in enhancing transparency and security. Blockchain can help combat fraud in digital advertising by verifying the legitimacy of clicks and ensuring ads are viewed by real people, not bots. It also offers new ways to manage consumer data, giving individuals more control over their information and how it's used by marketers.

Sustainable and Ethical Marketing

As consumers become more conscious of social and environmental issues, sustainable and ethical marketing practices will become increasingly important. Brands that demonstrate a genuine commitment to sustainability, social responsibility, and ethical behavior will gain a competitive edge. This trend requires marketers to reassess their strategies, from the sustainability of their products and packaging to the authenticity of their messaging.

Conclusion

The future of online marketing is poised for rapid transformation, driven by technological advances, changing consumer expectations, and a greater emphasis on privacy and ethics. Marketers must stay abreast of these trends, continuously adapting their strategies to remain competitive in a dynamic digital landscape. Embracing innovation, prioritizing the customer experience, and upholding ethical standards will be essential for success in the evolving world of online marketing.

2. Search Engine Optimization (SEO)

2.1 Fundamentals of SEO: How search engines work.

Search Engine Optimization, or SEO, is a cornerstone of effective online marketing. It's the art and science of enhancing website visibility in search engine results pages (SERPs) to attract organic traffic. Understanding SEO's fundamentals is essential for any digital marketer, content creator, or business owner aiming to establish a strong online presence. This chapter delves into the core aspects of SEO, offering insights into how search engines operate, the importance of keywords, and the basics of optimizing a website for better search rankings.

How Search Engines Work

At the heart of SEO is a deep understanding of how search engines work. Search engines like Google, Bing, and Yahoo use complex algorithms to crawl, index, and rank web pages. The process starts with crawling, where search engine bots, also known as spiders, scan the internet for content, reading the code/content of each URL they find. Next is indexing, where the crawled pages are stored in a database—a process akin to adding books to a library catalog. Finally, ranking determines the order of search results for a specific query, based on relevance and authority.

The Importance of Keywords

Keywords are the foundation of SEO. They are words or phrases that users enter into search engines when looking for information. Understanding the keywords your target audience uses is critical to optimizing your content and making it more visible in search results. Keyword research tools like Google Keyword Planner, SEMrush, and Ahrefs can help identify popular and relevant keywords in your niche. The goal is to incorporate these keywords naturally into your website's content, titles, meta descriptions, and URLs to improve your visibility for those terms.

On-page SEO

On-page SEO involves optimizing individual web pages to rank higher and earn more relevant traffic in search engines. This includes optimizing the content and the HTML source code of a page. Key elements of on-page SEO include:

- **Title Tags and Meta Descriptions**: These HTML elements provide an overview of your page's content. Including target keywords in your title tag and meta description can improve your page's relevance for those terms.
- **Header Tags**: Using header tags (H1, H2, H3) to structure content makes it easier for search engines to understand the hierarchy and relevance of your information.

- **Content Quality and Keyword Density**: Offering valuable, informative, and well-structured content is crucial. While keywords should be included naturally in your content, keyword stuffing, or overusing keywords, can penalize your rankings.
- **URL Structure**: SEO-friendly URLs should be concise, include target keywords, and be easy for search engines to crawl.
- **Alt Text for Images**: Descriptive alt text for images helps search engines understand the content of the images and can improve the visibility of your website in image search results.

Off-page SEO

While on-page SEO focuses on optimizing elements within your website, off-page SEO involves external factors that influence your site's authority and rankings. The primary component of off-page SEO is backlinks, which are links from other websites to yours. Backlinks from reputable and relevant sites can significantly boost your site's authority and rankings. Other off-page SEO strategies include social media marketing, guest blogging, and influencer outreach.

Technical SEO

Technical SEO refers to optimizing the technical aspects of your website to improve its visibility in search results. This includes:

- **Site Speed**: Faster websites provide a better user experience and are favored by search engines.
- **Mobile-friendliness**: With the increasing prevalence of mobile browsing, having a mobile-responsive website is crucial for SEO.
- **Secure Sockets Layer (SSL)**: Websites with SSL encryption (https://) are considered more secure and are often ranked higher than non-secure (http://) sites.
- **Structured Data Markup**: Using schema markup helps search engines understand the content of your website, potentially leading to richer search results (e.g., featured snippets).

The Evolution of SEO

SEO is an ever-evolving field, with search engines regularly updating their algorithms to provide better search results and combat spam. Staying updated with the latest SEO trends and algorithm changes is vital for maintaining and improving your website's search engine rankings.

Understanding the fundamentals of SEO is the first step toward mastering online marketing. By optimizing your website according to these principles, you can enhance your visibility in search engine results, attract more organic traffic, and ultimately achieve your business goals.

2.2 On-page SEO Techniques: Optimizing content and HTML.

On-page SEO is a cornerstone of search engine optimization that focuses on optimizing elements on your website to improve its visibility in search engine results pages (SERPs). This chapter delves into the various on-page SEO techniques that can significantly impact your site's ranking. By applying these strategies, you can create a website that is not only more appealing to search engines but also provides a better experience for your visitors.

Understanding On-page SEO

On-page SEO involves optimizing the content and HTML source code of a page. Unlike off-page SEO, which relates to links and other external signals, on-page SEO is fully under your control. It includes strategies to improve individual web pages, thereby increasing the site's search engine rankings and earning organic traffic.

Key Elements of On-page SEO

1. **Title Tags:** The title tag is one of the most critical on-page SEO elements. It's the headline that appears in search engine results and should be an accurate and concise description of your page's content. Best practices include using your primary keyword near the beginning of the title tag, keeping it under 60 characters to ensure it displays correctly on SERPs, and making it compelling to encourage clicks.
2. **Meta Descriptions:** Although meta descriptions don't directly influence rankings, they impact click-through rates (CTR). A well-crafted meta description provides a brief summary of the page's content and should include relevant keywords and a call to action. Keep it under 160 characters to ensure it's fully visible in search results.
3. **Header Tags:** Header tags (H1, H2, H3, etc.) help organize content for readers and search engines. Your H1 tag should contain your primary keyword and give a clear indication of the page content. Subsequent headers can be used to structure content and include secondary keywords.
4. **URL Structure:** URLs should be concise, include keywords, and be easy for search engines and users to understand. Use hyphens to separate words, keep URLs short, and avoid using unnecessary parameters or characters.
5. **Keyword Optimization:** Keywords should be naturally integrated into your content, titles, and meta descriptions. Focus on relevancy, search intent, and user experience rather than keyword density. Use long-tail keywords to target specific queries and semantic keywords to cover related concepts.

6. **Content Quality**: High-quality, unique content is vital for ranking well. Your content should provide value to your audience, answer their questions, and solve their problems. Engaging, well-researched content is more likely to earn links, shares, and keep visitors on your site longer.
7. **Image Optimization**: Images enhance user experience but can slow down your site if not optimized. Use descriptive file names, alt tags with relevant keywords, and compress images to reduce file size without losing quality. This not only helps with SEO but also accessibility.
8. **Mobile Responsiveness**: With mobile-first indexing, having a mobile-friendly website is crucial. Ensure your site is responsive, meaning it automatically adjusts to fit the screen size of the device it's being viewed on. Google's Mobile-Friendly Test tool can help you identify areas for improvement.
9. **Page Speed**: Site speed is a ranking factor for both desktop and mobile searches. Optimize your site's loading time by compressing images, minimizing code, leveraging browser caching, and using a content delivery network (CDN).
10. **Internal Linking**: Internal links help search engines understand the structure of your site and distribute page authority throughout it. Use descriptive anchor text and link to relevant content that provides additional value to your readers.

Implementing On-page SEO

Effective on-page SEO requires a strategic approach and ongoing effort. Start by auditing your current content and identifying areas for improvement. Prioritize pages with the potential to rank well and focus on optimizing those first. Remember, on-page SEO is not a set-it-and-forget-it task. It requires continuous monitoring, testing, and adjustment to align with evolving search engine algorithms and user behaviors.

By mastering on-page SEO techniques, you're not just optimizing for search engines; you're also enhancing the user experience. This dual focus can lead to higher rankings, increased traffic, and, ultimately, more conversions.

2.3 Off-page SEO Strategies: Backlinking and domain authority.

Off-page SEO, a pivotal aspect of search engine optimization, extends beyond the confines of your website, focusing on enhancing its reputation and authority from the outside. This chapter delves deep into the strategies that can significantly boost your site's visibility and ranking in search engine results pages (SERPs) by leveraging external factors. Off-page SEO is about building your site's perception in the digital ecosystem through quality backlinks, social media presence, and other external signals. Let's explore the critical components and actionable strategies of off-page SEO.

Understanding Off-page SEO

Off-page SEO refers to all the activities performed outside of your website to impact your rankings within search engine results. Unlike on-page SEO, which involves optimizing elements on your website (like content and HTML code), off-page SEO focuses on increasing the site's credibility and authority through other reputable places on the internet. This is primarily achieved through earning backlinks, creating social media buzz, and generating external attention.

The Power of Backlinks

Backlinks, also known as inbound links or external links, are links from other websites that point to your site. They are among the most critical factors for achieving high rankings. Here's why they matter:

- **Authority and Trust**: Search engines view backlinks as votes of confidence. A site with a high number of quality backlinks is considered authoritative and trustworthy.
- **Relevance and Context**: Backlinks from relevant and reputable sites within your industry or niche signal to search engines that your content is valuable and relevant to your field.
- **Diversity and Quality**: A diverse backlink profile with links from various authoritative domains can significantly boost your SEO performance. Quality over quantity is key, as links from high-authority sites are more beneficial than numerous links from low-quality sites.

Strategies for Building Quality Backlinks

1. **Content Marketing**: Create compelling, unique, and valuable content that naturally attracts backlinks. Infographics, research studies, and comprehensive guides are particularly effective.
2. **Guest Blogging**: Write articles for other reputable websites in your industry. This not only gets you a valuable backlink but also exposes your brand to a broader audience.
3. **Broken Link Building**: Identify broken links on other websites that you can replace with a link to relevant content on your site.
4. **Influencer Outreach**: Engage with influencers in your niche to get them to share your content or link back to your site.
5. **Competitor Analysis**: Analyze your competitors' backlink profiles to identify where they are getting their links from and target those sources too.

Social Media and Off-page SEO

While social media links typically do not influence rankings directly, they play a crucial role in off-page SEO by:

- **Increasing Online Visibility and Traffic**: Shares, likes, and comments improve visibility in your target audience, potentially leading to more organic backlinks.

- **Brand Building**: A strong social media presence helps build your brand, making your site more likely to be cited as a resource.

Other Off-page SEO Tactics

- **Forums and Online Communities**: Participating in relevant forums and online communities can help establish your expertise and encourage people to link to your site.

- **Local SEO and Citations**: For local businesses, having your business listed in reputable online directories is crucial. Ensure your business name, address, and phone number (NAP) are consistent across all listings.

- **Influencer Marketing**: Collaborating with influencers can lead to natural backlinks and increased brand visibility.

Monitoring and Analyzing Your Off-page SEO Efforts

Tracking your off-page SEO success is essential for understanding its impact on your overall SEO strategy. Use tools like Google Analytics, Ahrefs, or Moz to monitor backlinks, analyze the quality of linking domains, and measure traffic from social media and other external sources.

Conclusion

Off-page SEO is an integral part of a comprehensive SEO strategy. By focusing on building high-quality backlinks, leveraging social media, and engaging with the wider web community, you can significantly improve your site's authority and rankings in SERPs. Remember, off-page SEO is about establishing your site's reputation and trustworthiness, which takes time and consistent effort. By implementing these strategies diligently, you're setting your site up for long-term success in the digital landscape.

2.4 Technical SEO: Site architecture and crawlability.

Technical SEO refers to the optimization of website and server aspects to help search engine spiders crawl and index your site more effectively. This foundation enables your site to benefit from organic search rankings and user experience. Let's delve into the critical components of Technical SEO, exploring essential practices, tools, and considerations.

Understanding Technical SEO

At its core, Technical SEO encompasses the technical aspects of a website that affect its visibility in search engines. Unlike on-page SEO, which focuses on content and page optimization, Technical SEO is about improving site infrastructure. Ensuring that your website is designed, structured, and coded in a way that search engines can understand and rank it is paramount.

Key Components of Technical SEO

1. **Site Speed**: Page speed is a critical ranking factor for search engines. A faster website provides a better user experience and leads to higher engagement rates and conversions. Techniques to improve site speed include optimizing images, leveraging browser caching, minifying CSS, JavaScript, and HTML, and using a content delivery network (CDN).
2. **Mobile-Friendliness**: With the advent of mobile-first indexing, having a mobile-friendly website is essential. This means your site should look and function well on mobile devices. Responsive design, viewport settings, and touch-friendly navigation are critical factors in mobile optimization.
3. **HTTPS and Security**: Secure Sockets Layer (SSL) encryption is a must-have for websites. HTTPS not only protects your site's data and your users' privacy but also contributes positively to your site's ranking signals.
4. **Crawlability and Indexing**: Search engines must be able to crawl and index your site. This involves optimizing your robots.txt file to ensure search engines can access your content while excluding areas that should not be public. Utilizing XML sitemaps helps search engines discover and index your pages.
5. **Structured Data Markup**: Implementing structured data (Schema.org) helps search engines understand the content of your website and provide rich snippets in search results. This can enhance visibility and click-through rates.
6. **Canonical URLs and Duplicate Content**: Canonical tags help prevent duplicate content issues by specifying the "canonical" or "preferred" version of a web page. It's essential for managing similar content across multiple URLs.
7. **Website Architecture and Navigation**: A well-structured site with a logical hierarchy and clear navigation helps users and search engine bots find content easily. It involves organizing content in a clear manner, using breadcrumb menus, and creating an intuitive user interface.

Implementing Technical SEO

1. **Auditing Your Site**: Begin with a technical SEO audit to identify areas for improvement. Tools like Google Search Console, Screaming Frog SEO Spider, and SEMrush can provide insights into site speed, mobile usability, crawl errors, and more.
2. **Optimizing Site Performance**: Utilize tools like Google's PageSpeed Insights to analyze and improve your website's loading times. Consider upgrading your hosting solution if necessary.
3. **Ensuring Mobile Compatibility**: Use Google's Mobile-Friendly Test to check how easily a visitor can use your page on a mobile device. Implement responsive design principles to address any issues.

4. **Securing Your Site with HTTPS**: Obtain an SSL certificate and migrate your site to HTTPS. Ensure all resources on the page are also secured to avoid mixed content issues.
5. **Improving Crawlability**: Review and optimize your robots.txt file and submit your XML sitemap to search engines. Regularly monitor crawl stats in Google Search Console to identify and fix crawl errors.
6. **Using Structured Data**: Identify opportunities to implement Schema markup for products, reviews, articles, and more. Test your structured data using Google's Structured Data Testing Tool.
7. **Addressing Duplicate Content**: Implement canonical tags where necessary. Ensure your content management system (CMS) is configured to handle URL parameters correctly.
8. **Enhancing Site Architecture**: Simplify your website's structure. Ensure that no important content is buried too deep (more than three clicks away from the homepage), and utilize internal linking to help distribute page authority throughout your site.

Monitoring and Maintaining Technical SEO

Technical SEO is not a one-time task but an ongoing process. Regularly monitoring your site's health through analytics and webmaster tools, staying updated with search engine algorithms, and continuously optimizing can ensure your site remains competitive and compliant with best practices.

In conclusion, Technical SEO is a critical component of a comprehensive SEO strategy. By focusing on the technical elements that influence search engine rankings and user experience, you can build a strong foundation for your website's success in organic search results.

2.5 Measurability and SEO Tools: Utilizing analytics and monitoring tools.

In the ever-evolving landscape of search engine optimization (SEO), the ability to measure and analyze your efforts is crucial. Measurability in SEO refers to the process of tracking, analyzing, and interpreting various metrics to understand the performance of your SEO strategies. This chapter delves into the significance of measurability in SEO, the key metrics to monitor, and the most effective tools available to aid in these endeavors.

The Importance of Measurability in SEO

SEO is not a set-and-forget strategy; it requires constant monitoring and tweaking. The digital environment is dynamic, with search engines regularly updating their algorithms, competitors adjusting their strategies, and consumer behaviors shifting. Measurability allows marketers to gauge the effectiveness of their SEO tactics, identify areas for improvement, and make data-driven decisions to enhance their online visibility and ranking.

Key SEO Metrics to Monitor

To effectively measure the success of your SEO efforts, you need to focus on several critical metrics:

- **Organic Traffic**: The number of visitors coming to your site through search engine results pages (SERPs). An increase in organic traffic indicates successful SEO.

- **Keyword Rankings**: Positions of your website's keywords in SERPs. Tracking changes in rankings can help you understand your site's visibility for specific queries.

- **Click-Through Rate (CTR)**: The percentage of users who click on your website's link after seeing it in the search results. A higher CTR suggests that your title tags and meta descriptions are compelling and relevant.

- **Bounce Rate**: The percentage of visitors who leave your site after viewing only one page. A high bounce rate might indicate that your content is not meeting users' expectations.

- **Conversion Rate**: The percentage of website visitors who take a desired action, such as making a purchase or signing up for a newsletter. It helps gauge the effectiveness of your website in converting visitors into customers or leads.

- **Page Loading Speed**: Site speed affects user experience and is a ranking factor for search engines. Faster loading times can improve your rankings and user engagement.

- **Backlink Profile**: The quantity and quality of external sites linking back to your website. High-quality backlinks can boost your site's authority and rankings.

Essential SEO Tools

Several tools can help you track these metrics and provide insights into your website's SEO performance. Here are some of the most widely used SEO tools:

- **Google Analytics**: A free tool that provides comprehensive insights into your website's traffic, audience behavior, conversion rates, and more. It's essential for understanding how users interact with your site.

- **Google Search Console**: Another free tool from Google that offers valuable data about your site's visibility on Google SERPs. It helps you monitor your site's performance, understand your search traffic, and optimize your ranking.

- **SEMrush**: A comprehensive SEO tool that offers insights into your competitors' strategies, keyword research, backlink analysis, and much more. It's beneficial for both on-page and off-page SEO analysis.

- **Ahrefs**: Known for its backlink analysis capabilities, Ahrefs also provides tools for keyword research, competitor analysis, and site audits. It's invaluable for understanding your link profile and identifying opportunities for improvement.

- **Moz Pro**: Offers a suite of tools covering keyword research, link building, site audits, and page optimization insights. It's particularly useful for tracking your site's rankings and understanding the factors affecting your SEO performance.

Utilizing SEO Tools for Maximum Impact

To make the most out of these tools, it's important to:

- **Set Clear Objectives**: Define what success looks like for your SEO efforts. Whether it's improving keyword rankings, increasing organic traffic, or boosting conversions, having clear goals will help you measure progress effectively.

- **Regular Monitoring and Analysis**: SEO is not a one-time task. Regularly check your key metrics and adjust your strategies based on the data.

- **Combine Tools for Deeper Insights**: No single tool provides all the answers. Using a combination of tools can offer a more comprehensive view of your SEO performance.

- **Stay Updated**: SEO practices and tools evolve rapidly. Keeping abreast of the latest features and updates of these tools can provide you with a competitive edge.

Conclusion

Measurability is at the heart of successful SEO strategies. By effectively utilizing analytics and monitoring tools, marketers can gain valuable insights into their SEO efforts, refine their strategies, and achieve better rankings and visibility in search engine results. Remember, the goal is not just to gather data but to interpret it and take actionable steps that drive tangible improvements in your SEO performance.

3. Content Marketing

3.1 Developing a Content Strategy: Setting goals and analyzing the audience.

Developing a content strategy is the cornerstone of effective content marketing. It's a comprehensive plan that outlines how you will use content to meet your marketing objectives and satisfy your target audience's needs. A well-crafted content strategy encompasses everything from identifying your audience to measuring the success of your content efforts. This chapter delves into the steps and considerations necessary to develop a robust content strategy, ensuring your content marketing efforts are both purposeful and impactful.

Understanding Your Objectives

Before diving into content creation, it's crucial to define what you aim to achieve. Your objectives should align with broader marketing and business goals, whether that's increasing brand awareness, generating leads, or driving sales. Clear objectives will guide your content strategy, helping you to create content that's not only relevant and engaging but also effective in moving you towards your goals.

Knowing Your Audience

A deep understanding of your target audience is essential. This involves more than just demographic information; you need to grasp their challenges, interests, and behaviors. Creating audience personas can be a helpful exercise. These are semi-fictional representations of your ideal customers based on real data and some educated speculation about customer demographics, behavior patterns, motivations, and goals. Knowing your audience helps you tailor your content to speak directly to their needs and interests, making it more likely to resonate and engage.

Content Auditing

If you've been creating content for a while, conducting a content audit is a valuable step. This process involves reviewing all the content you've produced to determine what's working and what's not. Look for patterns in the performance of different types of content, topics, and distribution channels. An audit can reveal insights that inform your strategy, helping you focus on high-performing content types and topics.

Setting Up Your Content Pillars

Content pillars are the core themes or topics around which you'll build your content. These should reflect your audience's interests and your business's areas of expertise. Each pillar can be broken down into subtopics, providing a structured framework for generating content ideas. This approach ensures your content covers a broad range of topics relevant to your audience, all while staying aligned with your brand and objectives.

Content Types and Formats

Different types of content can serve different purposes and appeal to different audience preferences. Your strategy should include a mix of formats, such as blog posts, videos, infographics, podcasts, and social media posts. Consider the strengths of each format and how they can best serve your content pillars and audience preferences. For instance, complex topics might be best explained through an infographic or video, while in-depth discussions might be suited to blog posts or podcasts.

Content Creation and Workflow

Developing a streamlined content creation process is key to executing your strategy effectively. This includes planning who will research, write, design, and edit your content, as well as how content will be approved and published. Establishing a content calendar is also crucial, as it helps you plan and organize content around key dates, events, or product launches, ensuring a consistent and strategic approach to content publication.

Distribution and Promotion

Creating great content is only half the battle; you also need to get it in front of your audience. Your strategy should include plans for distributing your content across the most effective channels, whether that's your website, social media platforms, email newsletters, or other avenues. Consider also how you'll promote your content, using both organic methods and paid advertising to increase reach and engagement.

Measurement and Adjustment

Finally, determining how you'll measure the success of your content is critical. This involves setting key performance indicators (KPIs) that align with your objectives, such as website traffic, engagement metrics, lead generation, or sales attributed to content marketing efforts. Regularly review your content's performance against these KPIs, and be prepared to adjust your strategy based on what's working and what's not. This iterative process ensures your content strategy remains effective and aligned with your marketing goals.

Developing a content strategy is a dynamic process that requires ongoing attention and adaptation. By understanding your objectives, knowing your audience, and creating a structured approach to content creation and distribution, you can build a powerful content strategy that drives meaningful results for your business.

3.2 Content Creation: Crafting articles, videos, and infographics.

Creating compelling content is the cornerstone of any successful content marketing strategy. It's not just about filling your website with text or your social media with posts; it's about crafting valuable, relevant, and engaging content that resonates with your audience, fulfills their needs, and encourages them to interact with your brand. This chapter delves into the nuances of content creation, providing a comprehensive guide to developing content that captivates and converts.

Understanding Your Audience

Before you start creating content, it's crucial to understand who you're creating it for. This involves developing buyer personas, which are semi-fictional representations of your ideal customers based on market research and real data about your existing customers. Consider demographics, behavior patterns, motivations, and goals. The more detailed your personas, the more targeted and effective your content can be.

Types of Content

Content comes in various formats, and the right mix will depend on your audience's preferences and your marketing goals. Here are some of the most popular types:

- **Blog Posts**: Versatile and informative, blog posts can help boost SEO, provide value to your readers, and position your brand as an industry leader.
- **Videos**: With the rise of platforms like YouTube and TikTok, video content is more important than ever. It's engaging, shareable, and can convey a lot of information in a short amount of time.
- **Infographics**: These combine data and design to make complex information easy to understand and digest. They're highly shareable, making them excellent for social media.
- **Ebooks and Whitepapers**: For B2B marketing or when targeting customers in the decision-making stage, these provide in-depth insights on specific topics, helping generate leads.
- **Podcasts**: An increasingly popular format, podcasts allow you to reach your audience through engaging conversations and storytelling.

Content Creation Process

1. **Research and Ideation**: Every piece of content should start with thorough research. Look for gaps in your existing content, consider your SEO strategy, and think about what questions your audience might have. Tools like Google Trends, Answer the Public, and BuzzSumo can help identify popular topics and questions in your industry.
2. **Planning**: Once you have your ideas, plan your content calendar. This should include what type of content you'll create, when you'll publish it, and on what platforms. Consistency is key in content creation, so plan realistically based on your resources.
3. **Writing and Designing**: When creating your content, keep your audience and objectives in mind. Use a clear, engaging tone, and don't shy away from your brand's unique voice. For design, tools like Canva or Adobe Creative Suite can help you create professional-looking graphics and videos, even if you're not a designer.

4. **Editing and Proofreading**: Never underestimate the importance of this step. Editing and proofreading ensure your content is free of errors and aligned with your brand voice. Tools like Grammarly or Hemingway can help, but a human editor is invaluable for ensuring quality.
5. **Optimization**: Before you publish, optimize your content for search engines and social media. This includes using the right keywords, creating engaging titles and meta descriptions, and adding social sharing buttons.

Promoting Your Content

Creation is only half the battle; promotion is equally important. Share your content across your social media channels, email newsletters, and any other platforms where your audience is active. Consider paid promotion to reach a broader audience. Engage with your audience by responding to comments and feedback.

Measuring Success

Finally, track your content's performance using tools like Google Analytics, social media analytics, and email marketing metrics. Look at page views, social shares, time on page, and conversion rates to understand what works and what doesn't. Use these insights to refine your content strategy over time.

Creating effective content is a dynamic and ongoing process. It requires understanding your audience, experimenting with different formats, and continuously refining your approach based on performance data. With dedication and creativity, your content can attract, engage, and convert your target audience, driving success for your online marketing efforts.

3.3 Content Promotion: Leveraging distribution channels.

Promoting content is an essential step in the content marketing process because even the most informative, engaging, and well-produced content can fail to achieve its intended impact without effective distribution and promotion strategies. This chapter delves into the multifaceted approach to content promotion, covering various channels and techniques to ensure your content reaches your target audience, engages them, and drives the desired action.

Understanding Content Promotion

Content promotion involves using various tactics and channels to increase the visibility and reach of your content. The goal is to attract new visitors, engage current followers, and convert viewers into customers or supporters. Effective content promotion is not about spamming your audience but strategically placing your content where it can be discovered, appreciated, and shared.

Channels for Content Promotion

1. **Social Media**: Platforms like Facebook, Twitter, LinkedIn, Instagram, and Pinterest offer vast audiences and different ways to share content, from posts and stories to videos and live streams. Tailoring your content to each platform's audience and format can boost engagement and reach.
2. **Email Marketing**: Sending content directly to your subscribers' inboxes is a direct and personalized way to engage. Segmenting your email list allows for more targeted content promotion, improving relevance and response rates.
3. **Paid Advertising**: Using paid ads on social media, search engines, and other platforms can amplify your reach, especially to audiences that are hard to reach organically. PPC (pay-per-click) campaigns, display ads, and sponsored content are common strategies.
4. **Influencer Collaborations**: Partnering with influencers who have established audiences can introduce your content to new, engaged audiences. Choose influencers whose followers match your target demographic.
5. **SEO**: Optimizing your content for search engines increases its visibility in search results, making it more likely to be discovered by users looking for information in your niche.
6. **Guest Blogging**: Writing articles for other blogs or websites in your industry can introduce your brand and content to new audiences. It's also beneficial for building backlinks, which improve SEO.

Strategies for Effective Content Promotion

- **Know Your Audience**: Understand where your audience spends their time online and tailor your promotion strategy to those channels. Use analytics to refine your approach continuously.

- **Use a Content Calendar**: Planning your content promotion in advance helps ensure a consistent and strategic approach. A content calendar should include when and where each piece of content will be promoted.

- **Leverage Social Proof**: Encourage sharing by making your content easy to share and highlighting when others share your content. Testimonials, reviews, and user-generated content can also enhance credibility and engagement.

- **Repurpose Content**: Transform your content into different formats to maximize its reach and lifespan. A blog post can become a video, an infographic, or a series of social media posts.

- **Engage with Your Community**: Responding to comments, participating in discussions, and being active in relevant online communities can build relationships and encourage others to share your content.

- **Monitor and Analyze Performance**: Use tools to track how your promotion efforts are performing. Look at metrics like views, shares, time on page, and conversions to understand what's working and what's not.

- **Iterate and Optimize**: Use the insights gained from analytics to refine your content promotion strategies. Testing different approaches will help you understand what resonates with your audience and drives results.

Challenges in Content Promotion
Content promotion faces several challenges, including saturated markets, evolving algorithms on social media and search engines, and changing consumer behaviors. Staying informed about trends in digital marketing and being willing to adapt your strategies are crucial for overcoming these challenges.

Conclusion
Effective content promotion is not a one-size-fits-all approach but requires a mix of strategies, channels, and continuous optimization. By understanding your audience, leveraging multiple platforms, and analyzing your results, you can increase the reach and impact of your content. Remember, the goal of content promotion is to deliver value to your audience wherever they are, turning them from casual viewers into loyal followers and customers.

3.4 Content Optimization: Enhancing for SEO and usability.

Content optimization is a critical step in the content marketing process, ensuring that the material you produce is not only valuable and engaging for your audience but also discoverable via search engines. This chapter delves into the strategies and techniques for optimizing your content to improve both its search engine rankings and its usability for your audience.

Understanding Content Optimization
Content optimization involves refining and adjusting your content to maximize its effectiveness. This process includes implementing SEO best practices, improving readability, and ensuring that your content is accessible to as wide an audience as possible. The goal is to attract more traffic, engage readers, and ultimately drive conversions.

Keyword Research and Use
- **Identify Target Keywords**: Start by identifying the keywords and phrases that your target audience is using to find information related to your content. Tools like Google Keyword Planner, SEMrush, and Ahrefs can help you discover relevant keywords.
- **Incorporate Keywords Strategically**: Once you have your list of keywords, incorporate them into your content strategically. This includes placing them in your titles, headings, meta descriptions, and throughout the body of your content. However, avoid keyword stuffing, as it can negatively impact your SEO.

On-Page SEO Techniques

- **Title Tags and Meta Descriptions**: These are critical components of on-page SEO. Ensure your title tags are compelling and include your main keywords. Meta descriptions should provide a clear and concise summary of your content, enticing users to click through from the search results.
- **Headings and Subheadings**: Use headings (H1, H2, H3) to structure your content. This not only improves readability but also allows search engines to better understand the hierarchy and relevance of your content.
- **Internal Linking**: Link to other relevant pages and articles on your website. This helps distribute page authority throughout your site and keeps users engaged longer.

Enhancing Readability

- **Short Paragraphs and Sentences**: Keep your paragraphs and sentences short to improve readability. This makes your content easier to scan and digest, especially on mobile devices.
- **Use of Bullets and Lists**: Breaking down information into bullet points or numbered lists can significantly enhance the readability of your content, making it easier for readers to grasp key points.
- **Incorporate Visuals**: Images, videos, infographics, and other visual elements can break up text-heavy content, making it more engaging and easier to understand.

Content Accessibility

- **Alt Text for Images**: Always include descriptive alt text for images. This not only helps with SEO but also makes your content accessible to users who rely on screen readers.
- **Accessible Design**: Ensure that your content is accessible to all users, including those with disabilities. This includes using sufficient contrast ratios for text, ensuring navigability by keyboard, and providing captions for videos.

Mobile Optimization

With the increasing prevalence of mobile devices, ensuring your content is optimized for mobile is non-negotiable. This includes using responsive design to ensure your content looks great on all screen sizes, optimizing image sizes for quick loading, and minimizing intrusive pop-ups that can affect the mobile user experience.

Content Freshness

- **Regular Updates:** Updating your content regularly can improve its relevance and authority. This includes updating statistics, incorporating new information, and refreshing outdated sections.

- **Evergreen Content:** Focus on creating evergreen content that remains relevant and valuable over time. This type of content can continue to attract traffic and generate leads long after it's published.

Utilizing Analytics for Improvement

Finally, use web analytics to monitor your content's performance. Analyze metrics such as page views, bounce rate, and conversion rate to understand what's working and what's not. This data can provide valuable insights into how you can further optimize your content for better performance.

Content optimization is a continuous process. By implementing these strategies, you can improve the visibility, engagement, and effectiveness of your content, making it a powerful tool in your online marketing arsenal.

3.5 Measuring Success: Evaluating KPIs and ROI.

Evaluating the effectiveness of content marketing is crucial for understanding its impact on your business goals and for optimizing future strategies. This comprehensive guide to measuring success in content marketing will delve into the key performance indicators (KPIs) and return on investment (ROI) metrics that can help you gauge the efficiency of your content marketing efforts.

Understanding KPIs in Content Marketing

KPIs are quantifiable measures used to evaluate the success of a marketing campaign or strategy. In content marketing, KPIs help you understand how well your content is achieving its intended goals. These can range from increasing brand awareness and engagement to generating leads and boosting sales. Identifying the right KPIs is essential for meaningful analysis. Common content marketing KPIs include:

- **Website Traffic:** Measures the number of visitors to your content. It's a basic indicator of its reach and appeal.

- **Engagement Rate:** Includes metrics such as time spent on page, comments, shares, and likes. High engagement rates often indicate relevant and valuable content.

- **Lead Generation:** The number of leads generated through content, indicating its effectiveness in moving users along the sales funnel.

- **Conversion Rate:** The percentage of users who take a desired action after consuming your content, such as making a purchase or signing up for a newsletter.
- **SEO Performance:** Involves organic search rankings, click-through rates (CTR), and keyword performance, showing how well your content drives traffic via search engines.

Calculating ROI in Content Marketing

ROI is a critical metric for assessing the profitability of content marketing. It compares the cost of content creation and distribution against the revenue it generates. Calculating ROI can be challenging due to the difficulty in directly attributing sales to content marketing efforts. However, a basic formula to start with is:

ROI=Net Profit from Content Marketing−Cost of Content MarketingCost of Content Marketing×100ROI=Cost of Content MarketingNet Profit from Content Marketing−Cost of Content Marketing×100

- **Net Profit from Content Marketing:** This can be determined through sales attributed to content marketing campaigns, either via direct conversions or through a lead attribution model.
- **Cost of Content Marketing:** Includes all expenses related to content creation, distribution, and promotion, such as staff salaries, freelance fees, and marketing tools.

Advanced Techniques for Measuring Content Marketing Success

To gain deeper insights into your content marketing's effectiveness, consider the following advanced techniques:

- **Attribution Modeling:** Helps identify which content pieces contribute most to conversions or sales, by tracking the customer journey across multiple touchpoints.
- **Lifetime Value (LTV) Analysis:** Evaluates the long-term value of customers acquired through content marketing, providing insights into the profitability of retaining these customers.
- **Sentiment Analysis:** Goes beyond basic engagement metrics to assess the emotional response and perception of your brand, which can be indicative of future consumer behavior.
- **Competitive Benchmarking:** Involves comparing your content performance against that of your competitors, offering insights into your relative position in the market and areas for improvement.

Implementing a Framework for Continuous Improvement

Measuring success in content marketing is not a one-time task but a continuous process. Implementing a framework for regular analysis and refinement is key to sustaining and improving content marketing performance. This includes:

1. **Setting Clear Goals and KPIs**: Ensure your content marketing objectives are aligned with your overall business goals, and choose KPIs that accurately reflect these objectives.
2. **Regular Reporting and Analysis**: Create a schedule for regular reporting on KPIs and ROI, using analytics tools to gather and analyze data.
3. **Testing and Optimization**: Use A/B testing and other experimentation methods to continuously refine your content and strategies based on performance data.
4. **Stakeholder Communication**: Regularly communicate findings and insights to stakeholders and use their feedback to further refine your content marketing approach.

By effectively measuring the success of your content marketing through KPIs and ROI analysis, you can gain valuable insights into what works, what doesn't, and how to optimize your strategy for better results. This process of continuous evaluation and refinement is essential for achieving long-term success in content marketing.

4. Social Media Marketing

4.1 Overview of Social Media Platforms: Characteristics and audiences.

In the rapidly evolving digital landscape, social media platforms have emerged as pivotal channels for marketers aiming to engage with their target audiences directly and dynamically. Each platform possesses unique characteristics, user bases, and opportunities for brands. Understanding these nuances is crucial for crafting effective social media marketing strategies. This chapter delves into the diverse world of social media, providing a comprehensive overview of the most influential platforms, their key features, and how marketers can leverage these spaces for maximum impact.

Facebook: The Social Behemoth

Facebook remains one of the most expansive and versatile platforms, with over 2 billion monthly active users worldwide. It offers a rich array of marketing opportunities, from organic posts and community management in brand pages and groups to sophisticated advertising options through Facebook Ads. The platform's detailed targeting capabilities, based on user demographics, interests, and behaviors, allow for highly customized ad campaigns. Facebook is particularly effective for building community, enhancing brand loyalty, and driving traffic and conversions through both paid and organic strategies.

Instagram: A Visual Storytelling Powerhouse

Instagram, owned by Facebook (Meta), is a visually driven platform that has grown immensely popular, especially among younger demographics. It emphasizes photos, videos, and Stories, providing a highly engaging way to showcase products, share brand narratives, and connect with audiences through aesthetically pleasing content. Instagram's shopping features and the ability to link products in posts and stories have made it a vital platform for e-commerce brands. Utilizing Instagram effectively requires a keen eye for visual storytelling and an understanding of the platform's ever-evolving algorithm.

Twitter: The Pulse of Real-Time Conversation

Twitter is renowned for its real-time nature, making it an ideal platform for news, trends, and direct engagement with followers. With its character limit, the platform encourages concise and impactful messaging. Twitter is particularly effective for customer service, brand awareness campaigns, and engaging with trending topics through hashtags. The platform's immediacy and public conversational nature make it essential for brands looking to establish a voice in their industry and participate in wider conversations.

LinkedIn: The Professional Networking Giant

LinkedIn stands out as the premier professional networking platform, making it invaluable for B2B marketing, personal branding, and recruitment efforts. It offers unique content types, such as articles, posts, and videos, enabling professionals and brands to establish thought leadership in their industry. LinkedIn's advertising options are designed to target professionals based on job titles, industries, and professional interests, making it a powerful tool for B2B lead generation and brand positioning.

TikTok: The New Frontier of Viral Content

TikTok has surged in popularity, particularly among Gen Z and younger millennials, by offering a platform for short, engaging videos. It's known for its viral trends, music, and challenges, presenting a unique opportunity for brands to create highly shareable, entertaining content. TikTok's algorithm favors content that gains early engagement, making it possible for brands to achieve significant reach with creative strategies. Marketing on TikTok requires an authentic, creative approach that aligns with the platform's spontaneous and entertaining nature.

YouTube: The Video Content King

YouTube, the world's largest video-sharing platform, functions as a powerful tool for long-form content, tutorials, product reviews, and brand storytelling. With its vast user base, YouTube offers significant reach and the ability to build a dedicated audience through channel subscriptions. Effective YouTube marketing involves consistent content creation, SEO optimization for videos, and engagement through comments. The platform also offers targeted advertising options through Google Ads, making it a versatile channel for both organic and paid strategies.

Pinterest: The Visual Discovery Engine

Pinterest operates as a visual discovery engine where users can find inspiration, ideas, and products. It's particularly effective for driving website traffic and sales, especially for lifestyle, home decor, fashion, and food-related brands. Pinterest's unique format allows users to save (pin) content to boards, facilitating high engagement and shareability. Utilizing Pinterest for marketing requires a focus on high-quality, visually appealing images and strategic use of keywords for discoverability.

Snapchat: Engaging a Young Audience with Ephemeral Content

Snapchat caters to a predominantly younger audience, offering a platform for ephemeral content that disappears after viewing. Its features, such as Stories, filters, and Snap Ads, provide creative ways to engage users with short-lived content. Snapchat is particularly effective for behind-the-scenes content, exclusive offers, and influencer collaborations, appealing to the platform's desire for authenticity and spontaneity.

Strategic Integration Across Platforms

Understanding the unique attributes and audiences of each social media platform is the first step in developing a cohesive and effective online marketing strategy. Marketers should consider their brand's objectives, target audience, and content strengths when choosing which platforms to invest in. The key to success lies in crafting platform-specific strategies that leverage each channel's strengths, while maintaining a consistent brand voice and message across the digital landscape.

In conclusion, the dynamic and diverse nature of social media platforms offers a rich tapestry of marketing opportunities. By comprehensively understanding the nuances of each platform, marketers can craft strategic approaches that resonate with their target audiences, foster engagement, and drive meaningful results.

4.2 Building a Social Media Strategy: Planning and objectives.

In the dynamic realm of social media, a well-crafted strategy is the cornerstone of success. Without a clear plan, businesses and individuals alike can find themselves adrift in a sea of content, unable to reach their target audience effectively or achieve their marketing goals. This chapter delves into the essential steps and considerations for building a robust social media strategy that aligns with your overall marketing objectives.

Understanding Your Audience
The first step in crafting your social media strategy is to understand who your audience is. This involves creating detailed audience personas that outline demographics, interests, online behaviors, and pain points. Tools like Facebook Insights, Google Analytics, and Twitter Analytics can provide valuable data that helps in understanding who engages with your content and how they interact with your digital presence.

Setting Clear Objectives
Objectives are the guiding stars of your social media strategy. They should be specific, measurable, achievable, relevant, and time-bound (SMART). Common objectives include increasing brand awareness, driving website traffic, generating leads, enhancing customer engagement, and boosting sales. Each objective should directly contribute to your broader marketing and business goals.

Choosing the Right Platforms
Not all social media platforms are created equal, and not every platform will be suitable for your marketing needs. The choice of platforms should be influenced by where your target audience spends their time and the nature of your content. For example, visual products might perform better on Instagram or Pinterest, while B2B services might find more success on LinkedIn.

Content Planning and Creation
Content is the lifeblood of social media marketing. Your strategy should outline what types of content you will create, including posts, videos, infographics, and blogs. This

content should not only be engaging and high-quality but also aligned with the interests and needs of your audience. Additionally, a content calendar can help in organizing and scheduling your content to ensure a consistent and strategic presence.

Engagement and Community Building

Engagement is key to building a community around your brand. This means actively participating in conversations, responding to comments, and engaging with other users' content. Building a community also involves identifying and interacting with influencers and brand advocates who can amplify your message.

Monitoring and Analytics

To measure the success of your social media strategy, you need to track various metrics such as engagement rates, follower growth, website traffic from social media, and conversion rates. Tools like Hootsuite, Sprout Social, and Google Analytics can help track these metrics. Regular analysis allows you to understand what works, what doesn't, and how to adjust your strategy accordingly.

Adapting to Changes

Social media is an ever-evolving landscape. New platforms emerge, algorithms change, and user behaviors shift. A successful social media strategy must be flexible and adaptive, with regular reviews and updates to ensure it remains effective and relevant.

Legal and Ethical Considerations

It's crucial to be aware of the legal and ethical considerations when using social media for marketing. This includes respecting copyright laws, understanding the rules of each platform, and ensuring transparency with sponsored content and endorsements.

Conclusion

Building a social media strategy is a comprehensive process that requires understanding your audience, setting clear objectives, choosing the right platforms, and creating engaging content. It also involves active engagement, monitoring performance, and being adaptable to changes. With a well-defined strategy, businesses can harness the power of social media to reach their marketing objectives, build a loyal community, and drive significant growth.

4.3 Engagement and Community Building: Fostering interactions and loyalty.

In the realm of social media marketing, engagement and community building stand as pivotal pillars, not only fostering a sense of belonging among followers but also significantly amplifying brand visibility and loyalty. This chapter delves into strategies and practices for nurturing an active and engaged community on social media platforms.

Understanding Engagement on Social Media

Engagement on social media refers to any form of interaction between the brand and its audience. This includes likes, comments, shares, saves, and mentions. Engagement is a critical metric because it signifies that your content resonates with your audience, encouraging social platforms' algorithms to favor your content, thus increasing your reach and visibility.

Why Engagement Matters

- **Builds Relationships**: Regular interaction with your audience builds a relationship beyond the transactional. It humanizes your brand, making it more relatable and trustworthy.
- **Boosts Brand Loyalty**: Engaged customers are more likely to become repeat customers and brand advocates, sharing their positive experiences with others.
- **Enhances Visibility**: Algorithms prioritize content with higher engagement, showing your posts to a broader audience.
- **Provides Valuable Feedback**: Engagement is a direct line to customer feedback, offering insights into what your audience values.

Strategies for Boosting Engagement

- **Create Valuable Content**: Content should educate, entertain, or inspire your audience. It should be relevant to their interests and needs, encouraging them to interact.
- **Leverage Interactive Formats**: Polls, quizzes, Q&As, and live videos are interactive formats that prompt direct engagement from your audience.
- **Encourage User-Generated Content**: Share content created by your followers related to your brand. This not only provides you with authentic content but also encourages more users to share their own experiences.
- **Prompt Conversations**: Ask open-ended questions, solicit opinions, or start discussions relevant to your industry. Make sure to actively participate in these conversations.
- **Host Contests and Giveaways**: These can significantly increase engagement, but ensure they are aligned with your brand and valuable to your audience.

Building a Community

A community on social media is a group of individuals who share a common interest in your brand or industry. This community supports and engages with one another, driven by shared values and interests.

Key Elements in Community Building

- **Define Your Community's Purpose**: Clearly articulate what brings your community together. This could be a shared goal, interest, or value.

- **Create a Welcoming Environment:** Foster an inclusive atmosphere where members feel safe to express themselves and interact with others.
- **Regularly Engage with Your Community:** Be present and active. Respond to comments, participate in discussions, and acknowledge community members' contributions.
- **Provide Exclusive Value:** Offer your community something unique that they can't get elsewhere, such as exclusive content, early access to products, or special discounts.
- **Empower Members to Lead:** Identify active members and give them roles or responsibilities within the community. This not only lightens your load but also strengthens their loyalty to the community.

Measuring Success

To understand the impact of your engagement and community-building efforts, track key metrics such as:

- **Engagement Rate:** Measures the level of interaction your content receives relative to your number of followers.
- **Growth in Community Size:** Tracks the increase in your community members over time.
- **Sentiment Analysis:** Gauges the overall sentiment of the comments and interactions within your community.
- **Conversion Rate:** Determines how many of the engaged users take a desired action, such as making a purchase or signing up for a newsletter.

Best Practices and Real-World Examples

- Highlight success stories of community members using your products or services.
- Feature behind-the-scenes content that shows the human side of your brand.
- Implement regular "ask me anything" (AMA) sessions with your team or industry experts.

Engagement and community building are not about promoting your products but about creating meaningful connections. By prioritizing the needs and interests of your audience, you cultivate a loyal community that not only supports your brand but also contributes to its growth and success.

4.4 Advertising on Social Media: Utilizing paid promotions.

In the dynamic world of online marketing, social media advertising stands as a cornerstone, enabling brands to reach their target audience with unprecedented precision and scale. This chapter delves deep into the strategies, tools, and insights necessary for crafting successful social media advertising campaigns. We'll explore the nuances of platform selection, ad creation, targeting methodologies, budget optimization, and measuring success to empower marketers with the knowledge needed to excel in the digital arena.

Understanding Social Media Advertising Platforms

Each social media platform offers unique features, audience demographics, and advertising options, making platform selection a critical first step in the advertising process.

- **Facebook**: With the largest user base, Facebook excels in detailed targeting options, including interests, behaviors, and demographics, making it ideal for reaching a broad or highly specific audience.

- **Instagram**: Known for its visual appeal, Instagram is perfect for brands with strong visual content looking to engage younger demographics.

- **Twitter**: Offers rapid and real-time engagement, making it suitable for brands looking to participate in current events or trends.

- **LinkedIn**: The go-to platform for B2B advertising, LinkedIn allows targeting based on professional criteria such as industry, job title, and company size.

- **Pinterest**: A great platform for lifestyle and retail brands, Pinterest ads can drive high purchase intent traffic due to its discovery nature.

- **Snapchat**: With a younger user base, Snapchat is ideal for interactive and engaging ad formats that appeal to Gen Z and millennials.

Crafting Your Social Media Ad

Creating an effective social media ad requires a blend of creativity, strategic planning, and an understanding of your audience's needs and preferences.

- **Visuals**: High-quality images or videos that grab attention within a crowded feed.

- **Copy**: Concise, compelling text that conveys the value proposition and includes a clear call to action (CTA).

- **Value Proposition**: Clearly articulate what makes your product or service unique and why the audience should care.

- **Ad Formats**: Choose the right format (e.g., carousel, video, story ads) based on your campaign goals and the nature of your content.

Targeting Your Audience

The power of social media advertising lies in its targeting capabilities. Platforms offer various targeting options to ensure your ads are seen by a specific segment of users most likely to be interested in your product or service.

- **Demographic Targeting**: Age, gender, location, and language.

- **Interest-Based Targeting**: Users' interests, activities, and the pages they follow.
- **Behavioral Targeting**: Purchase behavior, device usage, and other actions.
- **Custom Audiences**: Target users who have previously interacted with your brand.
- **Lookalike Audiences**: Reach new users similar to your existing customers.

Budgeting and Bidding

Effective budgeting and bidding strategies are essential for maximizing return on investment (ROI) in social media advertising.

- **Setting a Budget**: Determine your overall budget based on campaign objectives and expected ROI.
- **Bidding Strategies**: Choose between cost per click (CPC), cost per impression (CPM), or cost per action (CPA) bidding, depending on your campaign goals.
- **Optimization**: Regularly adjust bids and budgets based on campaign performance to ensure optimal allocation of resources.

Measuring Success

To refine and improve future campaigns, it's crucial to measure and analyze the performance of your social media ads.

- **Key Performance Indicators (KPIs)**: Track metrics such as click-through rate (CTR), engagement rate, conversion rate, and cost per action (CPA).
- **Analytics Tools**: Utilize platform-specific analytics tools (e.g., Facebook Insights, Twitter Analytics) and third-party tools to gather data and insights.
- **A/B Testing**: Test different versions of your ads to determine which elements (e.g., imagery, copy, targeting) perform best.

Best Practices for Social Media Advertising

- **Stay Up-to-Date**: Social media platforms frequently update their advertising features and algorithms. Staying informed allows you to adapt and optimize your strategies accordingly.
- **Engage with Your Audience**: Respond to comments and messages to build a community around your brand.
- **Creative Consistency**: Ensure your ads align with your brand's voice and visual identity to build brand recognition and trust.
- **Leverage User-Generated Content**: Incorporate content created by your audience to enhance authenticity and engagement.
- **Continuous Learning**: The landscape of social media advertising is ever-evolving. Continuously analyze your campaigns' performance and learn from your successes and failures to refine your approach.

Social media advertising offers a powerful toolkit for brands to reach and engage with their target audience. By understanding the intricacies of different platforms, crafting compelling ads, targeting effectively, managing budgets wisely, and measuring results, marketers can drive significant business outcomes. As the digital landscape evolves, so too should your strategies, always aiming for creativity, engagement, and ROI optimization.

4.5 Analysis and Measurement: Tracking performance indicators.

In the ever-evolving landscape of social media marketing, the ability to analyze and measure the effectiveness of your campaigns is paramount. This chapter delves into the crucial aspect of performance tracking, focusing on the various metrics and tools that can help you understand the impact of your social media efforts. By the end of this chapter, you'll have a comprehensive understanding of how to use analysis and measurement to refine your strategy, enhance engagement, and ultimately achieve your marketing objectives.

Understanding Key Performance Indicators (KPIs)
Before diving into the specifics of analysis and measurement, it's essential to identify the Key Performance Indicators (KPIs) that are most relevant to your social media goals. These might include:

- **Engagement Rate**: This includes likes, shares, comments, and other forms of interaction that indicate how actively your audience engages with your content.
- **Reach and Impressions**: Reach measures how many unique users see your content, while impressions track the total number of times your content is displayed.
- **Click-Through Rate (CTR)**: The percentage of viewers who click on a link included in your post, indicating the effectiveness of your call to action.
- **Conversion Rate**: For campaigns aimed at driving specific actions, such as sales or sign-ups, this measures how many users took the desired action after interacting with your social media content.
- **Follower Growth**: Tracks the rate at which your social media following increases, providing insight into brand awareness and popularity.

Analytics Tools for Social Media
To measure these KPIs effectively, several analytics tools are at your disposal. Most social media platforms offer their own built-in analytics dashboards, such as Facebook Insights, Twitter Analytics, and Instagram Insights. These platforms provide a wealth of data on post performance, audience demographics, and engagement trends.

For a more comprehensive analysis that spans across multiple platforms, third-party tools like Hootsuite, Sprout Social, and Buffer offer advanced analytics features. These tools can aggregate data from various social media accounts, providing a holistic view of your digital presence and allowing for easier comparison of performance across platforms.

Conducting a Social Media Audit

A social media audit is a critical step in understanding your current performance and identifying areas for improvement. This process involves:

- **Reviewing your social media goals** to ensure they are still aligned with your overall marketing strategy.

- **Analyzing your audience** to understand their demographics, preferences, and behavior on social media.

- **Evaluating your content** to determine what types of posts generate the most engagement and why.

- **Comparing your performance** against competitors to benchmark your social media presence and identify opportunities to stand out.

Implementing a Data-Driven Strategy

With a clear understanding of your performance metrics and a comprehensive audit completed, you can move towards implementing a data-driven social media strategy. This involves:

- **Setting realistic and measurable goals** based on your audit findings and industry benchmarks.

- **Creating targeted content** that resonates with your audience and drives them towards your desired action.

- **Optimizing posting times** and frequency based on when your audience is most active and engaged.

- **Experimenting with different content formats** and strategies, using A/B testing to determine what works best.

- **Continuously monitoring and adjusting** your strategy based on real-time data and analytics.

Reporting and Communication

Effective analysis and measurement also involve regular reporting and communication of results to stakeholders. Creating monthly or quarterly reports that highlight key metrics, trends, and insights can help demonstrate the ROI of your social media efforts and secure ongoing support from your organization.

In conclusion, mastering the art of analysis and measurement in social media marketing is not just about tracking metrics; it's about using these insights to make informed decisions, personalize your approach, and continuously optimize your strategy for better results. By staying committed to a data-driven approach, you can ensure that your social media marketing efforts are aligned with your business goals and are effectively contributing to your brand's success.

5. Email Marketing

5.1 Setting Up an Email Marketing Campaign: Choosing tools and software.

Email marketing remains one of the most effective digital marketing strategies, offering unparalleled reach and potential for personalization. A well-executed email campaign can significantly boost engagement, conversions, and loyalty. This section delves into the initial phase of email marketing: setting up a campaign, focusing on the selection of tools and software, which lay the groundwork for success.

Understanding Email Marketing Platforms

The first step in setting up an email marketing campaign is choosing the right platform. An email marketing platform is software that provides tools for designing, sending, tracking, and optimizing email campaigns. It's essential to select a platform that aligns with your business needs, size, and marketing objectives.

Key features to look for include:

- **Automation and Drip Campaigns**: Automation tools enable you to send emails based on specific actions, dates, or engagement levels, ensuring timely and relevant communication with your audience.

- **List Management and Segmentation**: Effective list management capabilities allow you to organize your subscribers based on various criteria, enabling targeted and personalized campaigns.

- **Design and Customization**: A user-friendly email editor, with customizable templates, ensures that emails are both attractive and reflective of your brand.

- **Analytics and Reporting**: Insightful analytics help you track open rates, click-through rates, conversions, and more, offering a clear view of your campaign's performance.

- **Integration**: The ability to integrate with other marketing tools and software, such as CRM systems and social media platforms, enhances efficiency and data consistency.

Popular Email Marketing Platforms

Several email marketing platforms cater to a range of needs and budgets. Here are a few notable ones:

- **Mailchimp**: Known for its user-friendly interface, extensive template library, and robust analytics. Mailchimp suits businesses of all sizes, offering a free tier for small lists.

- **Constant Contact**: Offers comprehensive support and training, making it ideal for beginners. It features a wide array of integrations and a straightforward interface.

- **Sendinblue**: Highlights include advanced automation capabilities, transactional email support, and SMS marketing, alongside a flexible pricing model based on email volume.
- **Campaign Monitor**: Focuses on high-quality design and customization options, with powerful segmentation and personalization features for targeted campaigns.
- **ActiveCampaign**: Stands out for its advanced automation and CRM features, tailored for businesses looking to closely align marketing and sales efforts.

Setting Up Your Account
After selecting a platform, the next steps involve setting up your account:
1. **Sign Up and Configure Settings**: Provide your business details and configure basic settings, including sender name and email address, to ensure authenticity and compliance with email regulations.
2. **Import Your Email List**: If you have an existing subscriber list, import it into your chosen platform. Ensure you have consent from these contacts to comply with laws like GDPR.
3. **Segment Your List**: Organize your subscribers into segments based on demographics, behavior, or engagement levels to tailor your messaging effectively.
4. **Create Your First Campaign**: Utilize the platform's design tools to create your email. Focus on a clear message, compelling call-to-action (CTA), and a design that reflects your brand.
5. **Test and Send**: Before sending out your campaign, conduct tests to check for errors, mobile responsiveness, and overall appearance. Utilize A/B testing for subject lines or content variations to optimize engagement.

Legal Compliance
It's crucial to understand and adhere to email marketing laws and regulations, such as the General Data Protection Regulation (GDPR) in the European Union and the CAN-SPAM Act in the United States. These laws dictate the need for explicit consent from subscribers, provide guidelines for data handling, and establish requirements for unsubscribe options.

Conclusion
Setting up an email marketing campaign involves careful selection of the right tools and software, understanding platform features, importing and managing subscriber lists, creating and testing your first campaign, and ensuring legal compliance. By focusing on these foundational aspects, you can lay the groundwork for successful email marketing efforts that engage and convert your audience.

5.2 List Building and Segmentation: Collecting and organizing contacts.

List building and segmentation are cornerstone practices in effective email marketing. They involve collecting email addresses and other relevant information from potential and existing customers and organizing these contacts into specific groups for targeted communication. This chapter explores strategies for building a robust email list and segmenting it to enhance the relevance and effectiveness of your email campaigns.

Collecting Email Addresses
Opt-In Forms: The most ethical and effective way to gather email addresses is through opt-in forms on your website. These forms should be strategically placed where they're most visible to your visitors, such as on the homepage, blog posts, and landing pages. To encourage sign-ups, offer value in return, like exclusive discounts, ebooks, or valuable insights related to your niche.

Content Upgrades: Offer additional content like guides, checklists, or videos as an incentive for visitors to provide their email address. Content upgrades can significantly increase the conversion rate of your content marketing efforts by providing immediate value to your audience.

Social Media Channels: Utilize your social media profiles to promote sign-ups. This can be through direct links to your sign-up form, interactive posts that highlight the benefits of joining your list, or even through paid advertisements targeted at your ideal customer demographic.

Offline Methods: Don't overlook offline opportunities to grow your list, such as events, conferences, or in-store sign-ups. Ensure you have a quick and easy way for people to opt in, such as a signup sheet or a digital form accessible via a tablet.

Organizing Contacts
Once you've started collecting email addresses, the next step is to organize these contacts in a way that allows you to send them the most relevant and engaging content. **Segmentation**: This involves dividing your email list into smaller segments based on criteria such as demographics, purchase history, engagement level, and more. Effective segmentation can lead to more personalized email campaigns, improving open rates, click-through rates, and conversions.

Tagging: Apply tags to your contacts based on their behavior or how they entered your list. For example, if someone signed up to receive a free ebook, tag them with the ebook's name. This allows for precise targeting in future campaigns.

Lead Scoring: Implement a lead scoring system to prioritize contacts based on their engagement with your emails and website. This helps in focusing your efforts on leads that are more likely to convert.

Best Practices for List Building and Segmentation

Privacy and Compliance: Always comply with laws and regulations such as GDPR in the European Union. Make sure your opt-in forms include a checkbox for consent and clearly explain how you plan to use their email addresses.

Welcome Emails: Send a welcome email to new subscribers as soon as they sign up. This sets the tone for your relationship and can boost engagement from the outset.

Regular Cleaning: Periodically review your list to remove inactive subscribers or those who have opted out. This improves your deliverability rates and ensures your engagement metrics remain healthy.

Test and Refine: Continuously test different segments and personalized email content to see what resonates best with your audience. Use these insights to refine your segmentation strategy and improve the effectiveness of your campaigns.

Conclusion

Building and segmenting your email list are critical steps in developing a successful email marketing strategy. By collecting email addresses ethically and organizing contacts effectively, you can create personalized, targeted campaigns that resonate with your audience and drive results. Remember, the quality of your email list is more important than its size, and a well-segmented list is a powerful tool in any marketer's arsenal.

5.3 Email Design and Content: Personalizing and CTA crafting.

Creating compelling email content is more than just writing text and adding images. It involves a strategic blend of design, personalization, and clear calls to action (CTAs) that guide the recipient towards the desired outcome, whether that's making a purchase, signing up for a webinar, or following your brand on social media. This section dives into the essential elements of email design and content creation, focusing on personalization techniques and crafting effective CTAs.

Understanding Your Audience

The first step in designing an email campaign is understanding who your audience is. This involves segmenting your email list based on demographics, purchase history, engagement levels, and other relevant criteria. Personalization starts with knowing whom you're talking to, enabling you to tailor your message to meet their specific needs and interests.

The Role of Personalization

Personalization in email marketing goes beyond addressing the recipient by their first name. It's about delivering content that resonates with the individual's preferences and behaviors. Use data collected from previous interactions to segment your audience and customize your messages. For example, if a segment of your audience frequently purchases a particular product category, tailor your emails to highlight similar products or related offers.

Designing Your Email

The visual layout of your email plays a crucial role in engagement. A clean, organized design with a balance of text and visuals helps convey your message more effectively. Use a responsive design to ensure your email looks good on any device, from desktops to smartphones. Key elements to consider include:

- **Layout**: Use a grid layout to organize elements neatly. Keep important information and CTAs above the fold to catch the reader's attention immediately.

- **Colors and Fonts**: Choose colors and fonts that reflect your brand identity and ensure readability. Use contrasting colors for your CTA to make it stand out.

- **Images and Videos**: Incorporate high-quality images or videos to break up text and add a visual element to your message. Ensure they're optimized for quick loading times.

Crafting Compelling Content

The content of your email should be concise, engaging, and relevant to the recipient. Start with a catchy subject line that prompts the recipient to open the email. The body of your email should deliver on the promise of the subject line, providing valuable information or offers that meet the recipient's needs.

- **Subject Line**: Keep it short and enticing. Personalize it if possible.
- **Opening Line**: Make a strong first impression that encourages the reader to continue.
- **Body Content**: Use short paragraphs and bullet points for easy reading. Highlight key points or offers.
- **Visual Elements**: Use images or videos to complement your text and add visual interest.

Crafting Effective CTAs

Your CTA is the most critical element of your email. It's what turns a reader into a customer or a lead. Here are tips for crafting effective CTAs:

- **Be Clear and Concise**: Your CTA should tell recipients exactly what you want them to do. Use action-oriented language like "Buy Now," "Sign Up," "Learn More."

- **Create a Sense of Urgency:** Encourage immediate action with phrases like "Offer Ends Soon," "Limited Time Only."
- **Make it Visually Prominent:** Use a button or a contrasting color to make your CTA stand out from the rest of the email content.
- **Place it Strategically:** Include your CTA both above the fold and at the end of the email to catch the reader's attention regardless of how much they scroll.

Testing and Optimization

Finally, testing different elements of your email design and content is crucial for understanding what resonates best with your audience. A/B testing can be used to compare different subject lines, CTAs, layouts, and personalization strategies to see what performs better in terms of open rates, click-through rates, and conversions.

By focusing on personalization, thoughtful design, compelling content, and clear CTAs, you can create email campaigns that not only capture attention but also drive action. Remember, the goal of email marketing is to build relationships with your audience by providing value, and these strategies are key to achieving that goal.

5.4 Automation and Drip Campaigns: Streamlining for relevance.

In the realm of email marketing, the concepts of automation and drip campaigns stand out as pivotal strategies that significantly enhance the efficiency and effectiveness of communication with your audience. These techniques not only save time but also enable marketers to deliver highly targeted messages at optimal times, thus driving engagement and conversions. This section delves into the intricacies of automation and drip campaigns, offering insights into their implementation and optimization for maximum impact.

Understanding Email Automation

Email automation refers to the process of sending out emails to subscribers automatically, based on predefined triggers or schedules. This approach contrasts with traditional email blasts that are sent manually and indiscriminately to the entire mailing list. Automation leverages user data and behaviors to send personalized emails that are relevant to each recipient, thereby increasing the likelihood of engagement.

Key Components of Email Automation:

- **Triggers:** Actions taken by users, such as signing up for a newsletter, making a purchase, or abandoning a cart, that activate specific email responses.
- **Personalization:** Using subscriber data to tailor emails, addressing recipients by name and including content relevant to their interests and past behaviors.

- **Segmentation:** Dividing the email list into smaller groups based on criteria like demographics, purchase history, or engagement level to send more targeted communications.

Drip Campaigns Explained

Drip campaigns are a specific type of email automation characterized by a series of emails sent out at predetermined intervals. These emails "drip" valuable content, information, or promotions to subscribers over time, nurturing leads and building a relationship with the audience. Drip campaigns are designed to guide potential customers through the sales funnel, from awareness to decision-making and ultimately to conversion.

Strategies for Effective Drip Campaigns:

- **Welcome Series:** Introduce your brand and set the tone for future communications. Welcome emails are known for high open rates, making them an excellent opportunity to make a positive first impression.

- **Educational Content:** Provide valuable information related to your product or industry. This positions your brand as a helpful resource and builds trust with your audience.

- **Product Recommendations:** Based on past purchases or browsing behavior, send personalized product suggestions to encourage repeat business.

- **Re-engagement Campaigns:** Target subscribers who have become inactive or less engaged with content designed to recapture their interest.

Implementing Automation and Drip Campaigns

To implement email automation and drip campaigns effectively, marketers must follow a strategic process that encompasses planning, execution, and analysis.

Planning:

- **Define Objectives:** Clearly identify what you aim to achieve with your automation and drip campaigns, whether it's increasing sales, boosting engagement, or re-engaging dormant subscribers.

- **Segment Your Audience:** Utilize subscriber data to create segments. This ensures that the content of your automated emails and drip campaigns resonates with the specific interests and needs of each group.

- **Map Out the Customer Journey:** Understand the path your customers take from discovery to purchase and beyond. Tailor your email sequences to nurture leads at each stage of this journey.

Execution:

- **Choose the Right Email Marketing Tool:** Select a platform that offers robust automation and drip campaign features, along with analytics capabilities to measure performance.
- **Craft Compelling Content:** Ensure your emails provide value and speak directly to the recipient's needs and interests. Personalization and relevance are key to engaging your audience.
- **Test and Optimize:** Use A/B testing to refine subject lines, email content, and send times. Continuously analyze the performance of your campaigns and make adjustments as needed.

Measuring Success

The success of automation and drip campaigns can be evaluated through various metrics, including open rates, click-through rates (CTR), conversion rates, and overall ROI. These indicators help marketers understand how well their emails are performing and where there might be room for improvement. By closely monitoring these metrics, you can fine-tune your strategies to ensure your automation and drip campaigns consistently deliver results that align with your marketing objectives.

In conclusion, email automation and drip campaigns are powerful tools in the email marketer's arsenal, offering the ability to send timely, relevant, and personalized emails that drive engagement and conversions. By carefully planning, executing, and analyzing these campaigns, marketers can significantly enhance the effectiveness of their email marketing efforts, building stronger relationships with their audience and achieving their business goals.

5.5 Analysis and Improvement: Reviewing open and click rates.

In the realm of email marketing, the analysis and improvement phase is where the real magic happens. This subchapter delves into the crucial aspects of evaluating your email campaigns through open and click rates, offering actionable insights for optimization. Understanding and improving these metrics are pivotal for enhancing engagement, conversion rates, and ultimately, the success of your email marketing efforts.

Understanding Open and Click Rates

- **Open Rate** refers to the percentage of recipients who opened an email out of the total number of emails sent (excluding bounces). It's a primary indicator of how well your subject lines and sender reputation resonate with your audience.
- **Click Rate**, or click-through rate (CTR), measures the percentage of recipients who clicked on one or more links contained in an email. This metric is critical for assessing the effectiveness of your email content and calls to action (CTAs).

Analyzing Email Campaign Performance

1. **Benchmarking Your Metrics**: Start by comparing your open and click rates against industry averages. These benchmarks can vary significantly across different sectors, so it's important to reference data relevant to your niche.
2. **Segmentation Analysis**: Look into how different segments of your audience respond. Segmentation can be based on demographics, past purchase behavior, engagement level, or any other criteria relevant to your business. Identifying segments with higher or lower performance can guide you in tailoring your content more effectively.
3. **Trend Analysis**: Evaluate how your metrics evolve over time. Are your open rates improving? Is there a decline in click rates? Understanding these trends can help you pinpoint what works and identify areas requiring adjustment.

Improving Open Rates

- **Optimize Your Subject Lines**: Your subject line is the first impression. Test various approaches, such as personalization, questions, urgency, or curiosity-inducing statements to see what drives the best open rates.

- **Sender Name Recognition**: Use a sender name that your recipients recognize and trust. This could be your brand name, a specific person (e.g., "John from Company X"), or a combination of both.

- **Send Time Optimization**: Experiment with different sending times and days to find when your audience is most likely to open emails. Consider time zones for a geographically diverse audience.

Enhancing Click Rates

- **Compelling Content and Design**: Ensure your email content is engaging, relevant, and visually appealing. Use a clear and enticing CTA that encourages recipients to take the next step.

- **Personalization and Relevance**: Personalize your emails based on the recipient's interests, past behavior, or stage in the customer journey. The more relevant the content, the higher the likelihood of clicks.

- **A/B Testing**: Conduct A/B tests on various elements of your emails, including CTAs, layout, imagery, and messaging. This will help you understand what resonates best with your audience.

Utilizing Analytics Tools

Leveraging email marketing analytics tools can provide deeper insights into your campaign performance. These tools can track not just open and click rates, but also more advanced metrics like conversion rates, bounce rates, and the time spent on your website after clicking through. Integrating your email platform with web analytics tools can also help you track the customer journey beyond the initial click, offering a more comprehensive view of your email marketing effectiveness.

Actionable Insights for Continuous Improvement

- **Iterate Based on Data**: Use the insights gathered from your analysis to continually refine your email marketing strategy. This iterative process is key to staying relevant and engaging to your audience.

- **Feedback Loops**: Encourage and monitor feedback from your subscribers. Surveys, reply emails, and engagement on other channels can provide valuable qualitative data to complement your quantitative analysis.

- **Stay Updated on Best Practices**: Email marketing is an ever-evolving field. Stay informed about the latest trends, technologies, and regulatory changes to ensure your strategies remain effective and compliant.

By rigorously analyzing and improving upon your open and click rates, you can significantly enhance the performance of your email marketing campaigns. This ongoing process of testing, learning, and optimizing is fundamental to achieving sustained success in engaging your audience and driving conversions through email marketing.

6. Paid Advertising (PPC)

6.1 Basics of PPC: Understanding how PPC works.

Pay-Per-Click (PPC) advertising is a cornerstone of online marketing that allows businesses to place ads across digital platforms and pay only when a user clicks on them. This model offers the dual advantage of controlling advertising costs while maximizing exposure to targeted audiences. Understanding the basics of PPC is crucial for marketers looking to leverage this powerful tool effectively.

What is PPC?
At its core, PPC is an advertising model used on search engines, social media platforms, and other websites where advertisers can display ads linked to their products or services. The "pay-per-click" name comes from the billing structure—advertisers pay each time a user clicks on their ad. This model contrasts with other advertising models, such as cost-per-impression (CPM), where the advertiser pays per thousand ad views, regardless of user interaction.

Key Components of PPC
PPC advertising comprises several key components that work together to create successful campaigns:

- **Ad Platforms**: The most common platforms for PPC advertising include Google Ads, Bing Ads, and social media platforms like Facebook Ads and LinkedIn Ads. Each platform has its unique features and audience, allowing marketers to tailor their campaigns accordingly.

- **Keywords**: In search engine advertising, keywords are the foundation of PPC campaigns. Advertisers bid on keywords relevant to their target audience's search queries. The choice of keywords significantly influences the campaign's success, as it determines the ad's visibility to the intended audience.

- **Ad Copy and Creatives**: The text and visual elements of an ad must be compelling to attract clicks. Effective ad copy is clear, relevant, and includes a strong call-to-action (CTA). Creatives can include images, videos, or interactive elements, especially in social media advertising.

- **Landing Pages**: Once a user clicks an ad, they are directed to a landing page. This page should be optimized to convert visitors by providing valuable information, showcasing the advertised product or service, and guiding users toward a conversion action, such as making a purchase or signing up for more information.

- **Bidding and Budgeting**: Advertisers set a maximum bid for their ads, which is the highest amount they are willing to pay per click. Campaigns can be structured around different bidding strategies, such as focusing on maximizing clicks within a set budget or targeting specific conversion goals.

How PPC Works

The process behind PPC advertising involves several steps, from the initial setup to the ongoing management of campaigns:

1. **Campaign Setup**: Advertisers choose a platform, define their campaign goals, select target keywords, and create ad groups. Each ad group contains ads with similar themes targeting a specific set of keywords.
2. **Ad Auction**: When a user performs a search that includes keywords an advertiser has bid on, the platform's ad auction system determines which ads to display based on factors such as bid amount, ad relevance, and landing page quality.
3. **Ad Placement**: Ads that win the auction appear in the search engine's sponsored links or on the chosen social media platform. The placement can depend on the ad's rank in the auction, which is influenced by the bid and the ad's quality score—a metric that measures the relevance and quality of the ad and its landing page.
4. **Clicks and Conversions**: The ultimate goal of a PPC campaign is to generate clicks that lead to conversions. Conversions can vary, from a product purchase to a newsletter signup. Tracking conversions is essential for evaluating the campaign's success and ROI.

Benefits of PPC Advertising

PPC advertising offers several benefits, making it a popular choice among marketers:

- **Cost-Efficiency**: Since advertisers only pay when a user clicks on their ad, PPC can be a highly cost-effective way to drive traffic and conversions.

- **Targeting Capabilities**: PPC platforms offer advanced targeting options, including geographic, demographic, and device targeting, allowing advertisers to reach specific audiences.

- **Measurable Results**: With robust analytics, advertisers can track the performance of their PPC campaigns in real-time, allowing for quick adjustments to improve results.

- **Speed to Market**: Unlike organic search strategies, which can take time to yield results, PPC campaigns can be launched quickly, providing immediate visibility and results.

Understanding the basics of PPC is the first step toward mastering this essential online marketing tool. By carefully selecting platforms, keywords, and creative elements, and by continuously optimizing campaigns based on performance data, marketers can effectively use PPC to reach their target audiences and achieve their business objectives.

6.2 Setting Up Ad Campaigns: Working with Google Ads and social media ads.

Creating successful ad campaigns in today's digital landscape requires a deep understanding of various platforms and their unique advantages. This section dives into the intricacies of setting up ad campaigns, focusing on Google Ads and social media advertising, two of the most powerful channels for reaching potential customers online.

Understanding the Platforms

Google Ads operates on a pay-per-click (PPC) model, where advertisers bid on keywords and pay for each click on their advertisements. This platform is incredibly effective for capturing the intent of search queries, offering a direct route to people actively searching for solutions or products online.

Social Media Ads, on the other hand, leverage the extensive data social networks have on their users to allow advertisers to target their campaigns based on demographics, interests, behaviors, and more. Platforms like Facebook, Instagram, Twitter, and LinkedIn each offer unique opportunities to connect with audiences in a more personalized and engaging manner.

Campaign Objectives and Setup

1. **Defining Your Objectives**: The first step in setting up any ad campaign is to clearly define your objectives. Are you looking to drive traffic to your website, generate leads, increase sales, or boost brand awareness? Your objective will dictate your campaign strategy, including which platform to use, which ad formats, and how to allocate your budget.

2. **Choosing the Right Platform**: For direct intent, Google Ads is often the best choice. If your goal is more about brand awareness or targeting specific demographics or interests, then social media ads might be more effective.

3. **Account Setup**: For Google Ads, you'll need a Google account. For social media ads, you'll need an account on the respective platform's advertising manager, such as Facebook Ads Manager or LinkedIn Campaign Manager.

Keyword Research and Audience Targeting

1. **Google Ads Keyword Research**: Use tools like Google Keyword Planner to find keywords that are relevant to your business and have a high search volume but not overly competitive. Your aim is to bid on keywords that will bring the most relevant traffic to your site at the lowest cost.

2. **Social Media Audience Targeting**: Platforms like Facebook and Instagram offer detailed targeting options. You can segment audiences based on age, location, interests, behaviors, and more. Utilize these targeting options to tailor your message to the specific groups that are most likely to respond.

Creating Your Ads

1. **Ad Copy and Creative**: Whether for Google Ads or social media, your ad copy and creative should be compelling and directly aligned with your campaign objectives. For Google Ads, focus on including the target keywords in your ad text. For social media ads, use engaging visuals and videos to capture attention.

2. **Landing Pages**: Ensure that the landing page your ad points to is relevant, easy to navigate, and optimized for conversions. The message on the landing page should match the promise made in the ad to ensure a cohesive user experience.

Budgeting and Bidding

1. **Setting a Budget**: Determine your daily or campaign budget based on your overall marketing budget, the competitiveness of your keywords (for Google Ads), and the estimated reach of your target audience (for social media ads).

2. **Bidding Strategies**: Google Ads offers several bidding strategies, such as cost-per-click (CPC), cost-per-impression (CPM), or cost-per-acquisition (CPA), depending on your campaign objectives. Social media platforms also offer similar bidding options. Choose the strategy that aligns with your goals, whether it's maximizing clicks, impressions, or conversions.

Monitoring and Optimization

1. **Tracking Performance**: Use analytics and reporting tools provided by the platforms to track the performance of your campaigns. Key metrics to monitor include click-through rate (CTR), conversion rate, cost per click (CPC), and return on ad spend (ROAS).

2. **Optimization**: Continuously test and optimize your campaigns based on performance data. This can include adjusting your bid amounts, refining your target audiences, experimenting with different ad creatives, and tweaking your landing pages. The goal is to improve your campaign's efficiency and effectiveness over time.

Conclusion

Setting up ad campaigns on Google Ads and social media platforms can be a highly effective way to reach and engage your target audience. However, it requires careful planning, ongoing optimization, and a deep understanding of each platform's unique features and capabilities. By following the steps outlined above, advertisers can create impactful campaigns designed to meet their specific marketing objectives, whether they're looking to drive sales, generate leads, or increase brand awareness.

6.3 Keyword Research and Selection: Targeting effectively.

Keyword research and selection are fundamental steps in the process of search engine optimization (SEO) and pay-per-click (PPC) advertising. These steps are crucial for understanding how your target audience searches for your products, services, or content online. By identifying and implementing the right keywords, you can effectively optimize your website and ad campaigns to attract more relevant traffic, leading to increased conversions and success in your online marketing efforts.

The Importance of Keyword Research

Keyword research isn't just about finding words that receive a high volume of searches; it's about finding the words and phrases that your potential customers are using when they're looking for offerings like yours. It helps you understand the language of your target audience, including the variations and the context in which those terms are used.

This insight allows you to tailor your content, ads, and online strategies to align with the user's intent, increasing the likelihood of capturing their attention and fulfilling their needs.

Starting with Keyword Research

- **Understand Your Market:** Begin by developing a deep understanding of your market, your offerings, and the unique value proposition of your business. Consider the problems you solve and how customers might search for solutions to those problems.

- **Use Keyword Research Tools:** Leverage tools like Google Keyword Planner, SEMrush, Ahrefs, and Moz Keyword Explorer to find keywords related to your business. These tools provide data on search volume, competition level, and keyword difficulty, which can help you identify the most viable keywords to target.

- **Analyze Search Intent:** Search intent refers to the reason behind a search query. Understanding whether users are looking for information, comparing products, or ready to purchase can help you create more targeted content. Keywords can be categorized into four main types of intent: informational, navigational, commercial, and transactional.

- **Long-Tail Keywords:** While high-volume keywords may seem attractive, they often come with high competition. Long-tail keywords, which are longer and more specific phrases, tend to have lower search volumes but higher conversion rates. They allow you to target users who are further along in the buying process and more likely to convert.

- **Competitor Analysis:** Look at the keywords your competitors are targeting in their SEO and PPC efforts. This can give you insights into effective keywords and gaps in their strategies that you can exploit.

Implementing Your Keywords

- **SEO:** For SEO, incorporate your selected keywords naturally into your website's content, meta titles, meta descriptions, and URLs. Remember that keyword stuffing, or overusing keywords, can negatively impact your SEO efforts, so focus on creating user-friendly content that addresses the needs and questions of your audience.

- **PPC Campaigns:** In PPC campaigns, use your keywords to create relevant ad groups and ads. Match types (broad, phrase, exact) play a crucial role in how your ads are triggered by user searches. Crafting ad copy that includes your target keywords can improve your ad relevance and Quality Score, leading to better ad positions at lower costs.

- **Continuous Optimization:** Keyword trends can change over time, so it's essential to regularly review and update your keyword strategy. Use analytics tools to monitor the performance of your keywords in terms of traffic, conversions, and ROI. Adjust your strategy based on this data to continuously optimize for better results.

Conclusion

Effective keyword research and selection are not just about identifying the terms with the highest search volumes; they're about understanding your audience and how they search for what you offer. By carefully selecting keywords based on market understanding, search intent, and competitive analysis, and by continuously optimizing your implementation, you can significantly improve your online visibility, attract more qualified traffic, and achieve your marketing goals. Remember, the goal is to connect with your audience by speaking their language and meeting their needs, which starts with the right keywords.

6.4 Optimization and A/B Testing: Refining campaigns.

Paid Advertising, commonly known as Pay-Per-Click (PPC), is a powerful tool to reach your target audience. However, running successful PPC campaigns goes beyond just creating ads and targeting keywords. To maximize your ROI (Return on Investment) and manage your budget effectively, you need a well-structured approach. In this chapter, we'll delve into the various aspects of budgeting and ROI analysis within PPC campaigns.

Setting Your PPC Budget

Before you launch a PPC campaign, it's crucial to establish a clear budget. Your budget will determine the scope and scale of your advertising efforts. Here's how to set your PPC budget effectively:

Understanding Your Business Goals

- Begin by aligning your PPC goals with your overall business objectives. Are you looking to increase sales, generate leads, boost brand awareness, or something else? Define your key performance indicators (KPIs) based on these goals.

Keyword Research and Costs

- Conduct thorough keyword research to identify the keywords and phrases relevant to your business. Understand the cost-per-click (CPC) associated with each keyword, as this will impact your budget allocation.

Budget Allocation

- Allocate your budget among different campaigns, ad groups, and keywords strategically. High-performing keywords may warrant higher budgets, while testing new keywords may require smaller allocations.

Daily and Monthly Budget Limits

- Set daily and monthly budget limits to control your spending. This ensures that you don't overspend on a single day and can distribute your budget consistently over time.

ROI Tracking and Analysis

Once your PPC campaigns are live, it's essential to monitor and analyze their performance regularly. ROI analysis allows you to measure the effectiveness of your advertising efforts and make data-driven decisions. Here's how to conduct ROI analysis effectively:

Conversion Tracking

- Implement conversion tracking to measure actions that matter, such as form submissions, purchases, or sign-ups. Tracking conversions helps you determine which keywords and ads are driving valuable outcomes.

Cost-Per-Conversion (CPC)

- Calculate your cost-per-conversion for each keyword and campaign. This metric indicates how much you're spending to acquire each lead or customer. Lowering your CPC while maintaining quality is a key goal.

Return on Ad Spend (ROAS)

- ROAS measures the revenue generated for every dollar spent on advertising. For example, if you spend $100 on ads and generate $500 in revenue, your ROAS is 500%. Setting a target ROAS helps you optimize campaigns for profitability.

Click-Through Rate (CTR)

- Monitor CTR to assess ad relevance and audience engagement. A higher CTR often indicates that your ads are resonating with your audience. Low CTR may require ad copy or landing page optimizations.

Quality Score

- Google Ads assigns a Quality Score to keywords based on relevance, CTR, and landing page experience. A higher Quality Score can lead to lower CPC and better ad positioning.

A/B Testing

- Continuously run A/B tests to compare different ad creatives, landing pages, and keywords. Analyze the results to identify winning variations that improve ROI.

Attribution Models

- Understand how different attribution models (e.g., first-click, last-click, linear) impact ROI calculations. Choose the model that aligns with your business objectives and customer journey.

Adjusting Campaigns

- Use the insights from your ROI analysis to make data-driven adjustments. Allocate more budget to top-performing campaigns, pause underperforming ones, and refine ad copy and targeting.

Budget Optimization Strategies

To optimize your PPC budget and maximize ROI, consider the following strategies:

- **Bid Management**: Adjust keyword bids based on performance data. Increase bids for keywords with a high ROI and decrease bids for those with a low ROI.

- **Negative Keywords**: Continuously update your list of negative keywords to prevent ads from showing for irrelevant search queries.

- **Ad Scheduling**: Analyze the times of day and days of the week when your ads perform best. Adjust ad scheduling to allocate budget during peak hours.

- **Geographic Targeting**: Use geotargeting to focus your budget on areas with the highest conversion rates or where your target audience is most concentrated.

- **Ad Extensions**: Utilize ad extensions like sitelinks and callouts to enhance ad visibility and provide additional information.

- **Landing Page Optimization**: Ensure that your landing pages are optimized for conversions, offering a seamless user experience.

- **Ad Copy Testing**: Continuously test different ad copy variations to improve CTR and conversion rates.

- **Remarketing**: Implement remarketing campaigns to re-engage users who have previously visited your website but didn't convert.

- **Budget Reallocation**: Periodically review your budget allocation to allocate resources to the most profitable campaigns and keywords.

In conclusion, effective budgeting and ROI analysis are integral to the success of your PPC campaigns. By aligning your budget with your business goals, monitoring performance metrics, and optimizing your campaigns, you can achieve a strong ROI and make the most of your advertising budget in the competitive world of online marketing.

6.5 Budgeting and ROI Analysis: Managing costs and evaluating performance.

Paid Advertising, also known as Pay-Per-Click (PPC) advertising, is a dynamic and results-driven approach to reaching a target audience. While creating and managing PPC campaigns is essential, equally important is the ability to budget effectively and analyze Return on Investment (ROI). In this chapter, we delve deep into the crucial aspects of budgeting and ROI analysis in PPC advertising.

Setting Your PPC Budget Strategically

Setting a PPC budget is a pivotal step in ensuring the success of your paid advertising campaigns. Here's how you can approach it strategically:

Defining Your Objectives

1. Before allocating any budget, clearly define your campaign objectives. Are you looking to increase website traffic, generate leads, boost sales, or enhance brand visibility? Each objective may require a different budget allocation strategy.
2. Keyword Research and Selection
3. Conduct thorough keyword research to identify high-performing keywords relevant to your campaign goals. Understand the keyword competition and adjust your budget allocation accordingly. Highly competitive keywords may require a larger budget.
4. Daily and Monthly Budgeting
5. Determine your daily and monthly budget limits. Start with a daily budget that allows for adequate testing and optimization. Monitor your campaign's performance regularly and adjust the budget as needed to maximize ROI.
5. Ad Position and Bidding Strategy
6. Consider your desired ad position on search engine results pages (SERPs). Higher ad positions often require higher bids. Choose a bidding strategy, such as manual bidding or automated bidding, based on your goals and budget.
6. Allocating Budget to Different Campaigns and Ad Groups
7. If you're running multiple campaigns or ad groups, allocate your budget strategically based on their performance and priority. Allocate more budget to campaigns or ad groups that yield higher ROI.
7. Budget Flexibility

8. Maintain flexibility in your budget to adapt to unexpected changes, such as shifts in competition or seasonality. Allocate a portion of your budget for testing new strategies and keywords.

Measuring ROI in PPC Advertising

Once your PPC campaigns are running, it's essential to continuously measure and analyze ROI to ensure you're getting the most value from your budget. Here's how to do it effectively:

Tracking Conversions

Set up conversion tracking to measure actions that align with your campaign objectives. These actions could include website purchases, form submissions, or phone calls. Track both macro and micro conversions.

Calculating ROI

Calculate ROI by subtracting the total advertising costs from the total revenue generated through PPC campaigns. The formula for ROI is:

$$ROI = \frac{\text{Total Revenue} - \text{Total Advertising Costs}}{\text{Total Advertising Costs}}$$

A positive ROI indicates a profitable campaign, while a negative ROI signals that adjustments are needed.

Understanding Metrics

Analyze key PPC metrics such as Click-Through Rate (CTR), Conversion Rate, Cost Per Click (CPC), and Quality Score. These metrics provide insights into campaign performance and can guide optimization efforts.

A/B Testing and Optimization

Regularly conduct A/B tests to optimize ad copy, landing pages, and bidding strategies. Test variations to determine which combinations yield the best ROI. Continuous optimization is crucial for improving ROI over time.

Attribution Models

Consider different attribution models (e.g., first-click, last-click, linear) to understand the customer journey and how each touchpoint contributes to conversions. This can help in allocating budget more effectively.

ROI Analysis Tools

Utilize PPC analytics tools and platforms like Google Ads and Bing Ads to track and analyze ROI. These tools provide detailed insights into campaign performance and can assist in making data-driven decisions.

Strategies for Maximizing ROI

To achieve the highest possible ROI in PPC advertising, implement the following strategies:

- **Negative Keyword Management**: Continuously update and refine your list of negative keywords to prevent irrelevant clicks and wasted budget.
- **Ad Copy Optimization**: Craft compelling ad copy that aligns with user intent and encourages clicks and conversions.
- **Landing Page Optimization**: Ensure that landing pages are optimized for conversions, with clear calls-to-action and relevant content.
- **Quality Score Improvement**: Work on improving your Quality Score by enhancing ad relevance, click-through rates, and landing page experience.
- **Bid Management**: Adjust bids strategically to prioritize high-converting keywords and ad placements.
- **Ad Extensions**: Utilize ad extensions to provide additional information and encourage user engagement.
- **Remarketing**: Implement remarketing campaigns to re-engage previous visitors and boost conversions.

By implementing these strategies and continuously monitoring and optimizing your PPC campaigns, you can maximize ROI and make the most of your advertising budget.

Conclusion

Budgeting and ROI analysis are integral parts of a successful PPC advertising strategy. By setting clear objectives, allocating budgets strategically, measuring ROI effectively, and implementing optimization strategies, you can achieve a positive ROI and drive valuable results from your paid advertising efforts. PPC advertising, when managed with precision, can be a highly profitable component of your online marketing strategy.

7. Affiliate Marketing

7.1 Understanding Affiliate Marketing: Mechanics and benefits.

Affiliate marketing is a dynamic and lucrative online marketing strategy that has gained widespread popularity in recent years. This chapter provides an in-depth exploration of the fundamentals of affiliate marketing, shedding light on its mechanics, benefits, and the essential components that drive successful affiliate programs.

Introduction to Affiliate Marketing
Affiliate marketing is a performance-based marketing strategy in which businesses reward affiliates (publishers or partners) for driving traffic, leads, or sales to their websites or products through the affiliate's marketing efforts. It operates on a revenue-sharing model, making it a cost-effective and results-driven approach for both advertisers and affiliates.

Key Stakeholders in Affiliate Marketing
1. Advertisers (Merchants)
Advertisers are businesses or merchants who offer products or services and want to expand their reach through affiliate partnerships. They are the ones who set up affiliate programs, determine commission structures, and provide affiliates with marketing materials.

2. Affiliates (Publishers)
Affiliates are individuals or entities that promote products or services of advertisers through various marketing channels. Affiliates can be bloggers, website owners, social media influencers, email marketers, or even larger affiliate networks. They earn commissions based on the agreed-upon terms when their referrals lead to desired actions (e.g., a sale or lead generation).

3. Affiliate Networks
Affiliate networks serve as intermediaries between advertisers and affiliates. They provide a platform where advertisers can list their affiliate programs, and affiliates can discover and join these programs. Additionally, affiliate networks handle tracking, reporting, and payments, simplifying the management of affiliate partnerships.

How Affiliate Marketing Works
The affiliate marketing process involves several key steps:

1. Affiliate Program Setup
- Advertisers create an affiliate program, outlining commission structures, payment methods, and terms and conditions.

- They provide affiliates with unique tracking links or codes to monitor their referrals accurately.

2. Affiliate Promotion

- Affiliates choose products or services to promote based on their niche and target audience.
- They utilize various marketing channels, such as blogs, websites, social media, email newsletters, or paid advertising, to reach potential customers.
- Affiliates incorporate tracking links within their marketing materials to monitor conversions.

3. Visitor Clicks on Affiliate Link

- When a visitor clicks on an affiliate's tracking link, a cookie is stored on the visitor's device, identifying the affiliate as the referrer.
- The cookie typically has a predefined duration (e.g., 30 days), during which any subsequent conversions are attributed to the affiliate.

4. Conversion Occurs

- If the visitor takes the desired action, such as making a purchase or filling out a lead form, it is considered a conversion.
- The affiliate's referral is recorded, and the details are stored in the affiliate network's database.

5. Tracking and Commission Calculation

- Affiliate networks track conversions and calculate commissions based on the predefined terms.
- Commissions can be fixed amounts, a percentage of the sale, or other arrangements specified in the affiliate program.

6. Affiliate Payment

- Advertisers pay commissions to affiliates according to the agreed-upon schedule, which can be monthly, bi-weekly, or as specified in the affiliate program.

Benefits of Affiliate Marketing

Affiliate marketing offers numerous advantages for both advertisers and affiliates:

Benefits for Advertisers:

- **Cost-Efficient**: Advertisers pay only for actual results, making it a cost-effective marketing strategy.
- **Wider Reach**: Affiliate partnerships expand the reach of products or services to a broader audience.
- **Performance-Driven**: Advertisers can set clear performance goals and measure ROI effectively.

- **Scalability**: Affiliate programs can scale rapidly with the addition of more affiliates.
- **Low Risk**: Minimal financial risk since payment is based on performance.

Benefits for Affiliates:
- **Additional Revenue Stream**: Affiliates can earn passive income by promoting products or services.
- **Diverse Niches**: Affiliates can choose from a wide range of niches and products to promote.
- **No Product Creation**: Affiliates don't need to create or maintain products; they focus on marketing.
- **Flexible Work Environment**: Affiliates can work from anywhere with an internet connection.
- **Income Potential**: Successful affiliates can earn substantial commissions.

Legal and Ethical Considerations

Affiliate marketing operates within legal and ethical boundaries. It is essential for both advertisers and affiliates to comply with regulations, such as disclosing affiliate relationships and adhering to data protection laws.

Conclusion

Affiliate marketing is a versatile and performance-driven marketing strategy that benefits businesses, affiliates, and consumers. Understanding its core principles and mechanics is essential for building successful affiliate partnerships and harnessing its full potential in the ever-evolving digital marketing landscape.

In the subsequent chapters of this book, we will delve deeper into topics related to affiliate marketing, including setting up affiliate programs, selecting affiliates, campaign strategies, and measuring affiliate marketing success.

7.2 Setting Up an Affiliate Program: Choosing platforms and tools.

Affiliate marketing has become a powerhouse in the digital marketing landscape, allowing businesses to expand their reach and boost sales through partnerships with affiliates. Setting up an effective affiliate program is a critical step in harnessing the potential of this channel. In this chapter, we'll delve into the intricacies of establishing and managing a successful affiliate program.

Understanding Affiliate Marketing

Before diving into the setup process, it's crucial to grasp the fundamentals of affiliate marketing. Affiliate marketing involves collaborating with individuals or entities (affiliates) who promote your products or services in exchange for a commission on sales or leads they generate. This performance-based marketing strategy can be a win-win for both businesses and affiliates.

Defining Your Affiliate Program Objectives

Begin by outlining clear objectives for your affiliate program. What do you aim to achieve? Common goals include increasing sales, expanding brand awareness, and driving website traffic. Establishing these objectives will guide your program's structure and strategy.

Choosing the Right Affiliate Marketing Software

Selecting the appropriate affiliate marketing software is pivotal for the smooth operation of your program. Look for software that offers robust features such as tracking, reporting, commission management, and ease of integration with your e-commerce platform. Popular options include Post Affiliate Pro, PartnerStack, and Refersion.

Commission Structures and Payouts

Determining your commission structure is a critical decision. There are various models to consider, including:

- **Percentage of Sale**: Affiliates earn a percentage of the sale amount.
- **Fixed Amount per Sale**: A set commission for every sale.
- **Pay Per Lead (PPL)**: Affiliates receive payment for generating leads or sign-ups.
- **Pay Per Click (PPC)**: Compensation is based on the number of clicks generated.

The choice of commission model should align with your product pricing and business goals. Additionally, decide on the frequency of payouts, whether it's monthly, bi-weekly, or upon reaching a specific threshold.

Affiliate Recruitment and Onboarding

Recruiting the right affiliates is crucial for program success. Seek affiliates who align with your niche, target audience, and values. Reach out to potential affiliates through affiliate networks, industry forums, and social media platforms. Once affiliates are onboard, provide them with comprehensive training and resources to ensure they understand your products or services and can effectively promote them.

Compliance and Regulations

Compliance with legal and regulatory requirements is essential in affiliate marketing. Ensure that your affiliates adhere to ethical practices, disclose their affiliate relationship, and comply with data protection laws like GDPR. Create clear affiliate agreements outlining terms and conditions, code of conduct, and consequences for non-compliance.

Tracking and Attribution

Accurate tracking and attribution are the backbone of affiliate marketing. Implement tracking mechanisms to monitor affiliate-generated traffic and conversions. The use of tracking cookies or unique affiliate links helps attribute sales to the correct affiliate. Regularly audit and validate data to prevent fraud or discrepancies.

Performance Monitoring and Reporting

Continuously monitor your affiliate program's performance. Track key metrics such as sales, leads, conversion rates, and affiliate earnings. Utilize analytics tools and dashboards to gain insights into what's working and what needs improvement. Regularly share performance reports with affiliates to keep them motivated and informed.

Affiliate Program Promotion

Promote your affiliate program to attract more affiliates. Utilize your website, email marketing, and social media channels to create awareness. Offer incentives, bonuses, or tiered commission structures to motivate affiliates to perform better. Showcase success stories and testimonials from top-performing affiliates to inspire others.

Testing and Optimization

Optimizing your affiliate program is an ongoing process. Run A/B tests on creatives, landing pages, and promotional materials to identify what resonates best with your audience. Experiment with different commission structures and incentives. Continuously refine your program based on data-driven insights.

Managing Relationships

Building strong relationships with affiliates is crucial for program longevity. Regularly communicate with affiliates, provide them with support, and address their concerns promptly. Recognize and reward top-performing affiliates to foster loyalty.

Conclusion

Setting up an affiliate program requires careful planning, execution, and ongoing management. When done effectively, affiliate marketing can significantly contribute to your business's growth and revenue. By understanding the intricacies discussed in this chapter and continuously improving your program, you can harness the full potential of affiliate marketing as a valuable online marketing channel.

7.3 Selecting Affiliates: Partnering with the right entities.

In this chapter, we will explore the crucial aspects of collaborating with influencers in your online marketing strategy. Influencer marketing has emerged as a powerful tool for businesses to reach their target audience authentically and effectively. We will delve into the strategies, processes, and best practices for building successful influencer partnerships.

Introduction to Influencer Collaboration

Influencer marketing is a strategic alliance between brands and individuals who possess a significant and engaged online following within a specific niche or industry. This chapter will guide you through the steps required to initiate, manage, and maximize the potential of influencer collaborations.

Identifying the Right Influencers

Choosing the right influencers is pivotal to the success of your influencer marketing campaigns. In this section, we will discuss the criteria for selecting influencers that align with your brand's values, goals, and target audience. Key considerations include:

- **Relevance**: Ensure that the influencer's content and audience match your brand's niche and demographics.

- **Engagement**: Analyze an influencer's engagement rate (likes, comments, shares) to gauge their authenticity and influence.

- **Credibility**: Assess an influencer's credibility and reputation in their respective field.

- **Audience Size**: Consider the influencer's follower count, but remember that micro-influencers can be highly effective for niche markets.

Building Relationships with Influencers

Effective influencer partnerships are built on trust, transparency, and mutual benefit. We will cover the essential steps in establishing and nurturing relationships with influencers:

- **Initial Contact**: Approaching influencers with a clear and compelling proposal.

- **Negotiating Terms**: Discussing compensation, deliverables, and expectations.

- **Legal Agreements**: Drafting contracts to protect both parties' interests.

- **Content Collaboration**: Collaborating on content ideas and creation.

- **Feedback and Communication**: Maintaining open and consistent communication throughout the campaign.

Campaign Planning and Execution

Executing a successful influencer marketing campaign requires careful planning and execution. We will delve into the following aspects:

- **Campaign Objectives**: Defining clear and measurable goals for the influencer campaign.

- **Content Strategy**: Coordinating content creation and scheduling with influencers.

- **Distribution and Promotion**: Leveraging influencers' reach to amplify your brand's message.

- **Monitoring and Tracking**: Using analytics tools to measure campaign performance in real-time.

- **Adaptation and Optimization**: Making data-driven adjustments for improved results during the campaign.

Measuring the Impact of Influencer Marketing

In this section, we will explore the metrics and KPIs used to assess the success of your influencer marketing efforts. Key performance indicators include:

- **Engagement Metrics**: Likes, comments, shares, and click-through rates (CTR).
- **Conversion Rates**: Tracking how many users took desired actions after exposure to influencer content.
- **Brand Awareness**: Monitoring mentions, reach, and sentiment around your brand.
- **ROI and Cost-Effectiveness**: Calculating the return on investment and cost per acquisition (CPA).
- **Influencer Feedback**: Collecting insights and feedback from influencers for future improvements.

Challenges and Solutions

Influencer marketing is not without its challenges. We will address common issues and provide solutions, such as:

- **Fake Followers and Engagement**: Strategies to detect and avoid influencers with fake metrics.
- **Brand Alignment Issues**: How to navigate potential conflicts and misalignment.
- **Measurement Difficulties**: Overcoming measurement challenges and attribution modeling.
- **Maintaining Authenticity**: Ensuring that influencer content remains authentic and resonates with their audience.
- **Legal and Compliance Considerations**: Staying compliant with disclosure and advertising regulations.

Case Studies and Examples

To provide practical insights, we will present real-world case studies and examples of successful influencer marketing campaigns across various industries. These examples will illustrate the strategies and tactics discussed in this chapter and showcase the impact of influencer collaborations.

Conclusion

Influencer marketing can be a potent tool for your online marketing arsenal when executed strategically. This chapter has equipped you with the knowledge and strategies necessary to navigate influencer partnerships successfully. By identifying the right influencers, nurturing relationships, and measuring campaign impact, you can harness the full potential of influencer marketing to elevate your brand's online presence and engagement.

7.4 Affiliate Promotion Strategies: Effective methods.

Affiliate promotion strategies play a pivotal role in driving traffic, generating leads, and boosting sales. Affiliates, or partner marketers, act as intermediaries who promote products or services on behalf of businesses and earn commissions for successful conversions. In this chapter, we delve into the intricacies of affiliate promotion strategies, providing a comprehensive guide for both businesses and affiliates seeking success in this dynamic field.

Introduction to Affiliate Promotion Strategies

Affiliate marketing is a performance-based model that relies on partnerships between advertisers (merchants) and affiliates (publishers) to promote products or services. Understanding the fundamentals is essential before delving into the strategies.

The Affiliate Marketing Ecosystem

- **Advertisers (Merchants)**: Businesses that offer products or services and seek affiliate partners.

- **Affiliates (Publishers)**: Individuals or entities that promote advertiser products.

- **Affiliate Networks**: Intermediaries that facilitate affiliate relationships.

- **Consumers**: The target audience of affiliate promotions.

Identifying the Right Affiliate Partners
Affiliate Selection Criteria

- **Relevance to Niche**: Choose affiliates whose audience aligns with your product or service.

- **Quality of Content**: Assess the affiliate's website, blog, or platform for professionalism and credibility.

- **Audience Size and Engagement**: Analyze the affiliate's reach and level of audience engagement.

- **Track Record**: Review the affiliate's performance history, including conversion rates and ethical practices.

Crafting Effective Affiliate Marketing Campaigns
Setting Clear Goals

- **Define Objectives**: Determine what you aim to achieve, such as increased sales, leads, or brand awareness.

- **Target Metrics**: Identify key performance indicators (KPIs) for measuring success.

Developing Compelling Creative Assets

- **Banners and Ads**: Design eye-catching, persuasive creatives that affiliates can use.
- **Content Resources**: Provide affiliates with high-quality content, such as articles, videos, or infographics.
- **Branding Guidelines**: Ensure consistency in branding and messaging.

Creating Customized Affiliate Offers

- **Tiered Commission Structures**: Reward affiliates with higher commissions for exceptional performance.
- **Exclusive Promotions**: Provide unique offers to affiliates to differentiate their promotions.
- **Seasonal Campaigns**: Tailor offers to capitalize on seasonal trends and holidays.

Communicating Effectively with Affiliates
Building Strong Relationships

- **Regular Communication**: Keep affiliates informed about product updates, promotions, and changes.
- **Feedback Loop**: Encourage open dialogue for constructive feedback and improvement.

Providing Comprehensive Resources

- **Affiliate Portals**: Offer easy access to promotional materials, tracking tools, and reports.
- **Training and Support**: Provide educational resources and assistance as needed.

Performance Tracking and Reporting

- **Real-Time Analytics**: Implement tracking mechanisms to monitor affiliate-generated traffic and conversions.
- **Performance Reports**: Share detailed reports with affiliates, showcasing their impact on your business.

Compliance and Ethical Considerations
Affiliate Marketing Regulations

- **Disclosure**: Ensure affiliates disclose their partnership and any compensated promotions.
- **Privacy**: Comply with data protection laws when handling customer information.

- **FTC Guidelines**: Abide by the Federal Trade Commission's rules and guidelines for transparency.

Evaluating Affiliate Promotion Strategies

Continuous Optimization

- **A/B Testing**: Experiment with different promotional approaches to identify what works best.
- **Conversion Rate Optimization**: Analyze and improve landing pages and conversion funnels.
- **Affiliate Performance Reviews**: Regularly assess affiliate performance and adjust partnerships as needed.

Monitoring Fraud and Quality

- **Click Fraud Prevention**: Implement measures to detect and prevent fraudulent activity.
- **Quality Assurance**: Ensure that affiliate promotions align with your brand values and quality standards.

Conclusion

Affiliate promotion strategies are a dynamic and cost-effective way to expand your online marketing reach and increase revenue. By carefully selecting affiliate partners, crafting compelling campaigns, fostering strong relationships, and staying compliant with regulations, you can create a mutually beneficial ecosystem that drives success for both advertisers and affiliates. Continuous optimization and monitoring are essential for long-term growth and success in the affiliate marketing landscape.

7.5 Performance and Payment: Tracking and compensation models.

Understanding how performance is measured and how affiliates are compensated is crucial for both merchants and affiliate marketers. This chapter delves deep into the intricate details of performance metrics, compensation models, and best practices in the affiliate marketing industry.

Introduction

Affiliate marketing is a performance-based marketing model, meaning that affiliates earn commissions based on specific actions or results. The performance and payment structure in affiliate marketing is multifaceted and often varies between programs and industries. In this chapter, we will explore the intricacies of measuring performance and compensating affiliates effectively.

Performance Metrics

1. Click-Through Rate (CTR)
- **Definition**: CTR measures the percentage of clicks on an affiliate's promotional link relative to the total number of clicks.
- **Significance**: A high CTR indicates the effectiveness of the affiliate's promotional content.

2. Conversion Rate
- **Definition**: Conversion rate measures the percentage of visitors who take the desired action, such as making a purchase, after clicking on the affiliate's link.
- **Significance**: A high conversion rate demonstrates the affiliate's ability to drive quality traffic.

3. Average Order Value (AOV)
- **Definition**: AOV calculates the average amount spent by customers referred by the affiliate.
- **Significance**: A high AOV suggests the affiliate's audience generates substantial revenue.

4. Customer Lifetime Value (CLV)
- **Definition**: CLV estimates the total value a customer brings over their entire relationship with the merchant.
- **Significance**: Affiliates contributing to higher CLV are valuable for long-term success.

Compensation Models
1. Pay-Per-Sale (PPS)
- **Description**: Affiliates earn a commission for each sale generated through their referral.
- **Pros**: Aligns incentives with the merchant's goals, low financial risk for the merchant.
- **Cons**: Affiliates may focus on high-ticket items, potentially ignoring lower-value products.

2. Pay-Per-Click (PPC)
- **Description**: Affiliates earn a fee for each click on their affiliate link, regardless of subsequent actions.
- **Pros**: Attracts affiliates with strong traffic generation capabilities.
- **Cons**: Merchant may incur costs without guaranteed conversions.

3. Pay-Per-Lead (PPL)
- **Description**: Affiliates earn a commission for each lead they generate, typically through form submissions.
- **Pros**: Suitable for industries where direct sales are less common.
- **Cons**: Quality of leads may vary, leading to disputes.

4. Pay-Per-Click-Per-Sale (PPCPS)

- **Description**: Combines PPC and PPS models, where affiliates earn for both clicks and sales.
- **Pros**: Affiliates receive compensation even if a sale is not made immediately.
- **Cons**: Requires careful tracking and management to prevent abuse.

Affiliate Payment Structures

1. Commission Tiers

- **Description**: Reward affiliates with higher commissions as they achieve specific performance milestones.
- **Benefits**: Motivates affiliates to increase their efforts for greater rewards.
- **Challenges**: Requires effective tracking and communication to implement.

2. Performance Bonuses

- **Description**: Offer additional incentives or bonuses to affiliates who consistently perform exceptionally.
- **Benefits**: Encourages affiliates to excel and maintain a strong partnership.
- **Challenges**: Requires clear criteria and communication.

3. Recurring Commissions

- **Description**: Provide affiliates with commissions for recurring payments from referred customers (e.g., subscription services).
- **Benefits**: Builds long-term partnerships and incentivizes quality referrals.
- **Challenges**: Requires tracking customer behavior over time.

Payment Processing

1. Payment Methods

- **Description**: Discuss various payment methods, such as bank transfers, PayPal, and checks.
- **Recommendations**: Select payment methods that accommodate affiliates globally.
- **Timeliness**: Ensure prompt and reliable payments to maintain trust.

2. Payment Schedules

- **Description**: Determine when and how often affiliate payments will be disbursed (e.g., monthly, quarterly).
- **Transparency**: Communicate payment schedules clearly to affiliates.
- **Flexibility**: Accommodate affiliates with varying preferences.

Compliance and Monitoring

1. Compliance Guidelines

- **Description**: Establish clear guidelines for affiliates regarding promotional methods, disclosures, and ethical practices.
- **Monitoring**: Regularly audit affiliate activities to ensure adherence to guidelines.
- **Consequences**: Define consequences for non-compliance.

2. Fraud Prevention

- **Description**: Implement fraud detection measures to identify and mitigate fraudulent activities.
- **Techniques**: Use tracking technology and manual reviews to detect fraud.
- **Response**: Define a protocol for handling suspected fraudulent activities.

Conclusion

In the dynamic field of affiliate marketing, effective performance measurement and fair compensation models are paramount. This chapter has explored the key performance metrics, compensation models, and payment structures that enable merchants and affiliates to build mutually beneficial relationships. A well-structured affiliate program, aligned with performance and payment best practices, can be a valuable asset in a marketer's arsenal, driving growth and revenue for both parties.

8. Video Marketing

8.1 The Importance of Video in Online Marketing: Impact and reach.

the consumption of online content is rapidly evolving, and video has emerged as a dominant force in online marketing. With the proliferation of high-speed internet, mobile devices, and social media platforms, video marketing has become an integral part of any successful digital marketing strategy. In this chapter, we will delve into the significance of video in online marketing, exploring its impact, reach, and why it has become a crucial tool for businesses and brands.

Video's Role in Modern Marketing

Evolving Consumer Preferences
Consumer behavior has undergone a profound transformation in recent years. Audiences now prefer consuming information in video format over traditional text-based content. This shift is driven by the ease of consumption, as videos provide a more engaging and immersive experience. Studies have consistently shown that videos capture viewers' attention more effectively, making them a powerful medium for conveying messages.

Increased Engagement
One of the key reasons video has become essential in online marketing is its ability to drive higher engagement rates. Video content is inherently more shareable and likable on social media platforms, leading to increased brand exposure. Additionally, videos often generate more comments and discussions, facilitating audience interaction and strengthening the brand's online community.

Improved Conversion Rates
The impact of video on conversion rates cannot be overstated. Businesses incorporating video into their websites and landing pages often experience higher conversion rates. Whether it's a product demo, customer testimonial, or explainer video, well-crafted videos have the power to influence purchasing decisions and guide prospects through the sales funnel.

Video's Versatility in Marketing

Diverse Content Formats
Video is an incredibly versatile medium, allowing businesses to create a wide range of content formats. This versatility enables brands to tailor their messaging to different marketing objectives. From product showcases and tutorials to live streams and behind-the-scenes content, video adapts to various marketing needs.

Storytelling and Branding

Effective storytelling is at the heart of successful marketing, and video is a storytelling powerhouse. It allows brands to convey their narratives, values, and brand identity more effectively than text or static images. Videos provide a platform for emotional connections, making it easier for consumers to relate to and trust a brand.

SEO Benefits

Search engines prioritize video content in search results, making it a valuable tool for improving a brand's online visibility. When optimized with relevant keywords and metadata, videos enhance a website's SEO, leading to higher rankings. Additionally, video thumbnails in search results tend to attract more clicks, driving organic traffic.

Video's Impact on Social Media

Social Media Dominance

Social media platforms have evolved into video-centric spaces. Platforms like Facebook, Instagram, TikTok, and YouTube have witnessed a surge in video content consumption. Businesses that leverage these platforms for video marketing gain access to a vast and engaged audience.

Virality and Shareability

Videos on social media have the potential to go viral, reaching an audience far beyond a brand's immediate followers. Viral videos can catapult a brand into the spotlight, driving brand awareness and user-generated content. Shareable video content also encourages users to become brand advocates.

Measuring Video Marketing Success

Analytics and Metrics

Measuring the success of video marketing campaigns is essential for optimizing strategies. Businesses can track various metrics, including view counts, watch time, engagement rates, click-through rates, and conversion rates. These insights help refine video content and distribution strategies for better results.

A/B Testing and Optimization

A/B testing is a valuable technique in video marketing. Brands can experiment with different video formats, lengths, and content styles to determine what resonates best with their target audience. Continuous optimization based on A/B test results ensures that video marketing efforts remain effective and efficient.

Conclusion

In conclusion, video has become the cornerstone of modern online marketing. Its ability to engage, inform, and influence audiences is unparalleled, making it a vital tool for businesses aiming to thrive in the digital era. Understanding the importance of video in online marketing and harnessing its potential can significantly impact a brand's success in the competitive online landscape.

As we proceed through this chapter, we will explore in-depth strategies and techniques for creating engaging video content, optimizing it for search engines, and effectively promoting it across various digital platforms. Whether you're new to video marketing or looking to enhance your existing strategies, this chapter will provide the knowledge and insights you need to leverage the power of video in your online marketing endeavors.

8.2 Creating Engaging Video Content: Tips and techniques.

This chapter delves deep into the art and science of creating engaging video content, exploring every facet from conceptualization to execution.

Understanding the Importance of Video Content
Video content is a dynamic and immersive medium that can communicate ideas, evoke emotions, and establish strong connections with the audience. Understanding the significance of video content in the online marketing landscape is crucial before delving into the specifics of its creation.

The Impact of Video
Video's impact on online marketing cannot be overstated. Research consistently shows that video content is more engaging and memorable than text or static images. Videos have the ability to convey complex messages in a concise and relatable manner.

Video Across Platforms
Videos are versatile and can be used across various online platforms, including social media, websites, email marketing, and more. Tailoring your video content to each platform's unique audience and format is key to success.

SEO and Video
Search engines increasingly favor video content in search results, making it essential for improving visibility and driving organic traffic to your website. Optimizing video content for search engines is an integral part of video marketing.
Defining Your Video Strategy

Identifying Objectives
Before embarking on video creation, it's essential to define clear objectives. Are you looking to increase brand awareness, drive conversions, or educate your audience? Each objective requires a tailored approach.

Audience Research

Understanding your target audience is paramount. Conduct thorough research to identify their preferences, pain points, and interests. This data will inform your content and style choices.

Storytelling
Effective video content often relies on compelling storytelling. Craft a narrative that resonates with your audience, evokes emotion, and conveys your message authentically.

Planning the Production

Pre-production
Preparation is key to a successful video shoot. Create a detailed plan that includes scripts, storyboards, shot lists, and a production schedule. Securing the necessary equipment and personnel is crucial at this stage.

Filming Techniques
Mastering filming techniques is essential for producing high-quality videos. Consider aspects such as framing, lighting, camera angles, and composition to create visually appealing content.

Sound and Music
Audio quality is often underestimated but plays a significant role in viewer engagement. Ensure clear and crisp sound, and consider using music to enhance mood and pacing.

Editing and Post-production

Video Editing Software
Choose a professional video editing software that suits your needs. Familiarize yourself with its features to efficiently edit and enhance your video.

Editing Techniques
Video editing involves cutting, transitions, color correction, and adding graphics or animations. It's where your raw footage transforms into a polished final product.

Adding Value
Consider adding captions, subtitles, and calls to action (CTAs) to make your video more accessible and interactive. Ensure that your video aligns with your brand identity.

Optimization for Online Platforms

Format and Resolution
Different online platforms have specific requirements for video formats and resolutions. Optimize your video accordingly to ensure seamless playback and compatibility.

SEO for Video

Apply SEO techniques to your video content, including keyword optimization in titles, descriptions, and tags. Provide comprehensive metadata to help search engines understand your video's context.

Measuring Video Success

Key Performance Indicators (KPIs)
Establish KPIs that align with your video objectives. Common metrics include views, engagement (likes, comments, shares), conversion rates, and click-through rates (CTR).

Analytics Tools
Utilize analytics tools, such as Google Analytics and video-specific platforms like YouTube Analytics, to track and measure video performance. Analyze the data to refine your future video strategies.

Conclusion
Creating engaging video content is both an art and a science. It requires a deep understanding of your audience, strategic planning, skillful production, and meticulous optimization. When executed effectively, video content can be a game-changer in your online marketing efforts, fostering audience engagement and driving meaningful results.

8.3 Video SEO: Optimization for search engines.

Videos can convey information, entertain, and create lasting impressions. However, the value of a well-crafted video is only fully realized when it reaches its intended audience. This is where Video SEO (Search Engine Optimization) comes into play. In Chapter 8.3, we delve deep into the world of Video SEO, exploring its significance, strategies, and techniques to ensure that your videos rank high on search engines and captivate your audience.

Introduction
Video SEO is the practice of optimizing your video content to increase its visibility and rank on search engine results pages (SERPs). When done effectively, Video SEO can significantly enhance your online presence, drive traffic to your website, and improve brand recognition. In this chapter, we will explore the essential aspects of Video SEO, including keyword research, metadata optimization, and promotion strategies.

Understanding Video SEO

The Importance of Video SEO
Video SEO is crucial for several reasons:

- Enhanced Visibility

- Optimizing your videos for search engines makes them more discoverable. When potential viewers search for relevant topics, your optimized video is more likely to appear in the search results.
- Increased Traffic
- High-ranking videos attract more clicks and views, driving organic traffic to your website or video platform. This can lead to higher conversion rates and brand exposure.
- Improved User Engagement

Engaging videos that rank well can captivate your audience, encouraging them to stay longer on your website or channel. Longer watch times positively impact SEO.

Competitive Advantage
In a competitive digital landscape, Video SEO can set you apart from competitors and establish your authority in your niche.

Video SEO vs. Traditional SEO
While Video SEO shares similarities with traditional SEO, it has unique elements:
- Visual Appeal
- Videos must not only rank well but also engage visually. Factors like video quality, content relevance, and viewer retention are essential for Video SEO.
- Diverse Platforms
- Videos can be hosted on various platforms, including YouTube, Vimeo, and social media. Optimizing for multiple platforms requires tailored strategies.
- User Behavior

Understanding how viewers interact with videos, such as watch time and click-through rates, is crucial for Video SEO.

Key Elements of Video SEO

- **Keyword Research for Videos**
- Identifying Target Keywords
- Researching and selecting the right keywords is the foundation of Video SEO. Understand user intent and select keywords that align with your video content.
- Long-Tail Keywords
- Long-tail keywords can be highly effective for videos, as they cater to specific search queries and have lower competition.
- Competitive Analysis
- Analyze competitors' video keywords to identify opportunities and gaps in your strategy.

Optimizing Video Metadata

Video Titles
Craft compelling, keyword-rich titles that accurately represent your video content. Titles should be concise and engaging.

Video Descriptions
Write detailed, informative video descriptions that provide context and keywords. Include links to relevant resources.

Tags and Categories
Assign relevant tags and categories to your video to improve its discoverability.

Thumbnails
Create eye-catching thumbnails that encourage clicks and accurately represent the video's content.

Video Content Optimization
Quality and Relevance
Produce high-quality videos with relevant content that aligns with user expectations.

Video Length
Consider video length based on the content and audience preferences. Longer videos should maintain viewer engagement.

Transcriptions and Closed Captions
Providing transcriptions and closed captions can improve accessibility and SEO.

Technical Video SEO

Video Sitemaps
Generate video sitemaps to help search engines understand your video content and index it effectively.

Schema Markup
Implement schema markup to provide search engines with structured data about your video, enhancing its visibility.

Promotion and Distribution

Social Media Sharing
Leverage social media platforms to promote your videos, increasing views and engagement.

Embedding and Backlinking

Encourage others to embed your videos on their websites and create backlinks to improve authority.

Video Analytics and Monitoring

Tracking Performance

Utilize video analytics tools to monitor key metrics such as watch time, engagement, and conversion rates.

Conclusion

Effective Video SEO is an essential skill for modern marketers and content creators. It involves a multifaceted approach, from keyword research to content optimization and promotion. When done strategically, Video SEO can elevate your video content's visibility, engage your target audience, and drive valuable traffic to your digital assets. In this chapter, we've explored the significance of Video SEO and provided detailed insights and strategies to help you succeed in this dynamic and rewarding field.

8.4 Promoting Videos: Channels and strategies.

Video marketing is a powerful tool in the arsenal of digital marketers. It involves creating compelling video content and effectively promoting it to reach and engage with the target audience. In this chapter, we will delve into the intricacies of promoting videos as part of your online marketing strategy. We will explore various strategies, platforms, and techniques to ensure your videos receive the attention they deserve.

Understanding the Significance of Video Promotion

Before delving into the strategies, it's essential to grasp why video promotion matters in the digital landscape. Video has become a dominant medium for content consumption, and it offers several advantages:

1. Visual Appeal and Engagement

Videos are inherently engaging due to their visual and auditory elements. They can convey complex messages quickly and effectively, capturing the viewer's attention.

2. Improved SEO

Video content can enhance your website's search engine optimization (SEO) efforts. Search engines, such as Google, often prioritize video content in search results, making it a valuable asset for driving organic traffic.

3. Brand Awareness and Recognition

Well-promoted videos can significantly contribute to brand recognition. They help establish your brand identity and leave a lasting impression on viewers.

4. Social Sharing

Videos are highly shareable on social media platforms, increasing their potential reach. When viewers share your videos, it can lead to exponential exposure.

Crafting Compelling Video Titles and Descriptions

The first step in effective video promotion is creating attention-grabbing titles and descriptions. These elements are crucial for enticing viewers and improving search visibility.

- Title Optimization

- **Concise and Descriptive**: Craft titles that clearly convey the video's content and purpose.
- **Incorporate Keywords**: Include relevant keywords to improve search ranking.
- **Engaging Language**: Use compelling and action-oriented language to pique interest.

- Description Details

- **Synopsis**: Provide a brief summary of the video's content.
- **Keywords**: Include relevant keywords naturally in the description.
- **Links and Calls-to-Action (CTAs)**: Add links to your website or other relevant resources, along with CTAs encouraging viewers to take specific actions.

Leveraging Video SEO Techniques

Video search engine optimization (SEO) is a crucial aspect of video promotion. Optimizing your videos for search engines can significantly increase their discoverability.

- Video Metadata

- **Transcripts**: Include video transcripts to make your content accessible and to facilitate search engine indexing.
- **Tags and Categories**: Use relevant tags and categorization to assist search engines in understanding your video's content.

- Thumbnail Optimization

- **Eye-Catching Thumbnails**: Create custom thumbnails that are visually appealing and accurately represent the video's content.
- **High Resolution**: Ensure thumbnails are of high quality to enhance professionalism.

Utilizing Social Media Platforms

Social media is a powerful channel for video promotion due to its extensive user base and sharing capabilities.

- Native Uploads
  - **Platform-Specific Formats**: Tailor your video content to each social media platform's preferred format and dimensions.
  - **Engagement Features**: Encourage likes, shares, and comments to increase visibility within social networks' algorithms.
- Paid Advertising
  - **Boosted Posts**: Invest in paid advertising to promote your videos to a broader audience.
  - **Audience Targeting**: Use detailed targeting options to reach your ideal demographic.

Email Marketing Integration

Integrating videos into email marketing campaigns can significantly increase engagement rates.
- Video Thumbnails in Emails
  - **Clickable Thumbnails**: Embed clickable video thumbnails within email content.
  - **Compelling Previews**: Use engaging preview images to entice recipients to watch the video.

Collaborations and Influencer Partnerships

Collaborating with influencers or other brands can expand your video's reach and credibility.

- Identifying Suitable Partners
  - **Relevance**: Choose partners whose audience aligns with your target demographic.
  - **Authenticity**: Ensure that partnerships feel authentic and resonate with both audiences.

- Co-Promotion Strategies
  - **Cross-Promotion**: Promote videos on each other's platforms for mutual benefit.
  - **Influencer Endorsement**: Have influencers endorse and share your video content.

Measuring Video Performance

After implementing video promotion strategies, it's essential to measure performance to gauge effectiveness.

- Key Metrics
  - **Views**: Track the number of video views.

- **Engagement**: Monitor likes, comments, shares, and click-through rates (CTR).
- **Conversion Rate**: Analyze how video views translate into desired actions, such as sign-ups or purchases.

- A/B Testing
- **Content Variations**: Experiment with different video content and promotion methods.
- **Optimization**: Continuously optimize your video promotion strategies based on A/B test results.

Conclusion

Effective video promotion is a multifaceted process that involves optimizing video content, leveraging SEO techniques, utilizing social media platforms, integrating videos into email marketing, collaborating with influencers, and measuring performance. By implementing these strategies and continuously refining your approach, you can harness the full potential of video marketing and reach a broader audience while achieving your marketing goals.

8.5 Measuring Success: Analyzing video performance.

The real value of video marketing lies not only in creating captivating content but also in effectively measuring its success. In this chapter, we delve deep into the intricacies of measuring the performance and impact of your video marketing campaigns.
Key Performance Indicators (KPIs)

Video marketing success begins with defining and tracking the right Key Performance Indicators (KPIs). These KPIs are essential metrics that provide insights into the effectiveness of your video campaigns. Let's explore some of the most critical KPIs in detail:

1. **View Count**: The view count is the simplest and most apparent metric, representing the number of times your video has been viewed. However, it's essential to understand that a high view count doesn't necessarily equate to success, as it doesn't reflect viewer engagement or conversions.

2. **Watch Time**: Watch time measures the total amount of time viewers have spent watching your video. It's a valuable metric for assessing how engaging and informative your content is. Longer watch times indicate that viewers find your video compelling and stay engaged.

3. Engagement Rate: Engagement rate includes metrics like likes, shares, comments, and click-through rates (CTRs). High engagement rates signify that your video has resonated with the audience and encouraged them to take action, whether it's liking, sharing, or leaving a comment.

4. Conversion Rate: Ultimately, the success of your video marketing campaign often hinges on conversions. A conversion can be defined as a desired action taken by a viewer after watching the video, such as signing up for a newsletter, making a purchase, or filling out a contact form. Tracking the conversion rate allows you to assess how well your video drives viewers toward your goals.

5. Click-Through Rate (CTR): CTR measures the percentage of viewers who clicked on a call-to-action (CTA) or a link included in your video or video description. A high CTR suggests that your video effectively drives viewers to take the desired action, such as visiting your website or landing page.

6. Audience Retention: Audience retention shows how well your video maintains viewer interest throughout its duration. It provides insights into the points where viewers tend to drop off. By identifying these drop-off points, you can optimize your content to keep viewers engaged until the end.

7. Social Shares: The number of times your video has been shared on social media platforms is a testament to its shareability and relevance. Social shares expand your video's reach and can lead to increased visibility.

Analytics Tools and Platforms
To effectively measure these KPIs, it's crucial to leverage analytics tools and platforms designed for video marketing. Here are some widely used tools and their functionalities:

1. Google Analytics: Google Analytics provides in-depth insights into website traffic and user behavior, including the performance of videos embedded on your site. It can track metrics like watch time, conversion rates, and audience demographics.

2. YouTube Analytics: For videos hosted on YouTube, YouTube Analytics offers a comprehensive dashboard with data on views, watch time, engagement, and demographics of your viewers. It also provides information about traffic sources and viewer devices.

3. Social Media Insights: Social media platforms like Facebook, Instagram, and Twitter offer built-in analytics tools to monitor video performance on their respective platforms. These tools provide metrics on views, shares, comments, and engagement rates specific to each platform.

4. Video Hosting Platforms: If you use third-party video hosting platforms like Vimeo or Wistia, they often offer detailed analytics, including heatmaps that show where viewers are most engaged in your video.

A/B Testing and Optimization

Measuring success isn't solely about collecting data; it's also about using that data to refine your video marketing strategy. A/B testing is a powerful method for optimization. It involves creating two versions of a video with slight variations (e.g., different thumbnails, titles, or CTAs) and testing them to see which performs better in terms of KPIs.

When conducting A/B tests, it's essential to:

- Clearly define the objective of the test.
- Randomly assign viewers to the test groups.
- Monitor the results and statistically analyze the data.
- Implement the winning version based on the test outcome.

Optimization should be an ongoing process, with continuous testing and refinement to improve video performance.

Conclusion

In the realm of video marketing, success goes beyond mere views; it's about engaging your audience, driving conversions, and continually improving your strategy. By focusing on the right KPIs, utilizing analytics tools, and embracing A/B testing and optimization, you can measure the true impact of your video marketing efforts and create content that resonates with your target audience.

9. Influencer Marketing

9.1 The Landscape of Influencer Marketing: Overview and trends.

This chapter delves into the intricate landscape of influencer marketing, offering a comprehensive understanding of its significance, historical context, and current trends. Introduction

Influencer marketing is a marketing strategy that leverages the influence and reach of individuals, often referred to as influencers, to promote products, services, or brands. It has gained immense popularity in recent years due to its ability to establish authenticity, create meaningful connections, and drive consumer engagement. This section provides an introduction to the core concepts of influencer marketing and its relevance in the contemporary digital landscape.

The Evolution of Influencer Marketing
In order to grasp the depth of influencer marketing, it is essential to trace its evolution over time. Historically, influencer marketing can be traced back to celebrity endorsements in traditional advertising. However, the digital age has given rise to a new breed of influencers who have cultivated their audiences on platforms such as social media, YouTube, and blogs. This section explores the historical roots of influencer marketing and its transition into the digital era.

The Role of Influencers
Understanding the pivotal role that influencers play in this marketing strategy is crucial. Influencers are individuals who have established credibility and authority within a specific niche or industry. They possess the ability to sway the opinions and behaviors of their followers, making them valuable assets for brands seeking to connect with a target demographic. This section delves into the various types of influencers, from micro-influencers with niche followings to macro-influencers with mass appeal.

The Mechanics of Influencer Marketing
A fundamental comprehension of how influencer marketing operates is essential for successful implementation. This section provides a detailed breakdown of the mechanics involved in influencer marketing campaigns. It covers the identification and selection of influencers, negotiation of partnerships, content creation, and campaign execution. Additionally, it explores the legal and ethical considerations that brands must navigate when engaging in influencer collaborations.

Trends and Innovations
Influencer marketing is a dynamic field that constantly evolves to adapt to changing consumer behaviors and technological advancements. Staying ahead of the curve is

crucial for marketers seeking to harness the full potential of influencer partnerships. This section explores the latest trends and innovations in influencer marketing, including the rise of virtual influencers, the impact of live streaming, and the integration of augmented reality (AR) and virtual reality (VR) experiences.

Measuring Success and ROI

Measuring the success of influencer marketing campaigns is a critical aspect of evaluating their effectiveness. Marketers must assess key performance indicators (KPIs) and calculate return on investment (ROI) to determine the impact of their efforts. This section delves into the various metrics and tools available for measuring influencer marketing success, including engagement rates, reach, conversion rates, and attribution modeling.

Case Studies and Best Practices

Learning from real-world examples is invaluable in influencer marketing. This section presents a series of case studies highlighting successful influencer marketing campaigns across different industries. These case studies serve as practical illustrations of effective strategies and offer insights into best practices for achieving desired outcomes in influencer collaborations.

Challenges and Pitfalls

While influencer marketing offers numerous advantages, it is not without its challenges and potential pitfalls. This section identifies common hurdles faced by brands and influencers alike, including issues related to authenticity, transparency, and audience fatigue. Strategies for mitigating these challenges are discussed to help marketers navigate the complex influencer landscape.

Ethical Considerations

Maintaining ethical standards in influencer marketing is crucial for preserving trust and credibility. This section explores the ethical considerations that both brands and influencers must prioritize, including the disclosure of sponsored content, transparency in partnerships, and responsible content creation.

Future Outlook

To conclude, this chapter provides a glimpse into the future of influencer marketing. It discusses emerging trends, potential disruptions, and the evolving role of influencers in the digital marketing ecosystem. Understanding the trajectory of influencer marketing can help marketers prepare for what lies ahead and adapt their strategies accordingly. In summary, this chapter offers a comprehensive exploration of the influencer marketing landscape, from its historical roots to its current trends and future prospects. It equips readers with the knowledge and insights necessary to navigate this dynamic field and harness the power of influencer partnerships in their online marketing efforts.

9.2 Finding and Selecting Influencers: Criteria and approaches.

Businesses and brands recognize the value of collaborating with individuals who have a significant and engaged online following. This chapter explores the critical aspects of finding and selecting influencers for your influencer marketing campaigns.

Introduction

Influencers are individuals who have established credibility and authority within a specific niche or industry. They possess the ability to sway the opinions and behavior of their audience, making them valuable partners for brands aiming to reach a target demographic effectively. However, the process of finding and selecting the right influencers can be intricate and requires careful consideration.

Understanding Your Campaign Objectives

Before embarking on the journey of finding influencers, it is imperative to have a clear understanding of your campaign objectives. What are you trying to achieve with influencer marketing? Are you looking to increase brand awareness, drive sales, or promote a new product? The answers to these questions will shape your influencer selection criteria.

Defining Your Target Audience

Your influencer marketing success hinges on your ability to resonate with your target audience. Thus, it is essential to define your target audience thoroughly. Consider demographics, interests, behaviors, and preferences. By identifying your audience's characteristics, you can pinpoint influencers whose followers align with your target demographic.

Identifying Relevant Niches

Influencers often operate within specific niches. To maximize the impact of your campaign, you should identify relevant niches that intersect with your brand or product. Research different niches to uncover those that are most likely to yield positive results for your campaign.

Researching Influencers

The process of finding influencers necessitates thorough research. Start by exploring social media platforms, blogs, YouTube channels, and other online spaces where influencers congregate. Use hashtags, keywords, and search tools to identify potential candidates.

Qualitative Assessment

Qualitative assessment involves evaluating influencers based on subjective criteria. Consider factors such as content quality, authenticity, engagement, and alignment with your brand values. Review their content to ensure it resonates with your brand's messaging.

Quantitative Assessment

Quantitative assessment involves analyzing specific metrics related to an influencer's online presence. These metrics may include the number of followers, likes, comments, shares, and views. While numbers are essential, it's crucial to focus on the quality of engagement rather than just quantity.

Audience Analysis

Examine an influencer's audience demographics, including age, gender, location, and interests. Ensure that their followers match your target audience to maximize the relevance of your campaign.

Content Review

Review the influencer's past content to gain insights into their style, tone, and messaging. Assess whether their content aligns with your brand's image and values. Additionally, verify if they have previously collaborated with competitors or similar brands.

Reach Out and Build Relationships

Once you've identified potential influencers, it's time to reach out and build relationships. Initiate contact through personalized messages, expressing your interest in collaboration. Building a rapport with influencers can lead to more successful and authentic partnerships.

Negotiating Terms

Negotiating terms and agreements with influencers is a crucial step in the selection process. Discuss compensation, deliverables, timelines, and campaign objectives. Ensure that both parties are aligned on expectations to avoid misunderstandings later.

Legal and Ethical Considerations

Influencer marketing involves legal and ethical considerations. Familiarize yourself with advertising regulations, disclosure requirements, and privacy laws in your jurisdiction. Ensure that influencers adhere to these regulations when promoting your brand.

Measuring Impact

Finally, establish key performance indicators (KPIs) and measurement tools to track the impact of your influencer marketing campaigns. Analyze metrics such as engagement rates, click-through rates, conversion rates, and ROI to evaluate the campaign's success.

In conclusion, finding and selecting influencers for your influencer marketing campaigns is a meticulous process that demands attention to detail and alignment with your brand's goals. By understanding your objectives, defining your target audience, and conducting comprehensive research, you can identify influencers who will authentically promote your brand and resonate with your audience. Building strong relationships and ensuring legal compliance are equally vital steps in creating successful influencer partnerships.

9.3 Collaborating with Influencers: Setting up and managing.

This chapter delves deep into the intricate process of collaborating with influencers to orchestrate impactful campaigns. We explore the nuances of building influencer relationships, campaign execution, and the art of measuring and analyzing outcomes.

The Significance of Influencer Marketing
In the contemporary digital landscape, influencer marketing has evolved into a dynamic force. It capitalizes on influencers' credibility and reach to forge authentic connections with audiences. The chapter begins by elucidating the importance of influencer marketing in an era where consumers crave genuine interactions.

Identifying the Right Influencers
Selecting the appropriate influencers is pivotal to the success of any influencer marketing campaign. We offer a comprehensive guide on how to identify influencers aligned with your brand's objectives. This includes considerations such as niche relevance, audience demographics, and engagement rates.

Establishing Collaborative Relationships
Building fruitful relationships with influencers necessitates a strategic approach. We delve into the intricacies of influencer outreach, negotiations, and contractual agreements. The chapter also navigates the complexities of compliance with regulations and disclosure guidelines.

Crafting Creative and Authentic Campaigns
The heart of influencer marketing lies in crafting compelling campaigns that resonate with the audience. We explore the creative aspects of campaign ideation, content collaboration, and storytelling. Learn how to maintain brand integrity while allowing influencers the creative freedom to connect authentically with their followers.

The Art of Campaign Execution
Executing an influencer marketing campaign demands precision and coordination. This section offers insights into campaign management, content scheduling, and the technical aspects of collaboration. Discover how to ensure the seamless integration of influencer-generated content into your broader marketing strategy.

Measuring and Analyzing Campaign Performance

In the digital age, data is a treasure trove that informs decision-making. Dive deep into the intricacies of measuring and analyzing influencer marketing campaign performance. We explore the key performance indicators (KPIs) that matter most, from engagement metrics to conversion rates.

Leveraging Advanced Analytics Tools

To gain a competitive edge, it is essential to harness advanced analytics tools. Uncover the potential of data-driven insights in influencer marketing. We discuss the integration of analytics platforms, sentiment analysis, and ROI attribution models.

Navigating Challenges and Pitfalls

Influencer marketing is not without its challenges. This section equips you with the knowledge to anticipate and address common pitfalls. Learn how to mitigate issues related to influencer authenticity, negative publicity, and crisis management.

The Future of Influencer Marketing

As influencer marketing continues to evolve, we offer a glimpse into the future. Explore emerging trends such as micro-influencers, virtual influencers, and AI-powered influencer identification. Gain foresight into the ever-changing landscape of influencer marketing.

Case Studies and Success Stories

The chapter concludes with real-world case studies and success stories. Dive into examples of brands that have masterfully leveraged influencer marketing to achieve remarkable results. These practical illustrations serve as a source of inspiration and guidance for your influencer marketing endeavors.

In essence, this chapter provides a comprehensive roadmap for collaborating with influencers in the realm of online marketing. From influencer identification to campaign execution and performance analysis, it equips you with the knowledge and insights needed to navigate the dynamic and impactful world of influencer marketing.

9.4 Campaign Creativity and Execution: Unique content and collaborations.

Influencer marketing has evolved into a sophisticated and dynamic strategy that harnesses the power of influential individuals to promote brands, products, or services.

In this chapter, we delve deep into the art and science of crafting influencer marketing campaigns that resonate with audiences, drive engagement, and deliver measurable results. We will explore various aspects of campaign creativity and execution, emphasizing the importance of strategic planning and collaboration with influencers.

Understanding the Campaign Objective

Before embarking on an influencer marketing campaign, it's crucial to define clear and measurable objectives. Understanding the desired outcomes will guide campaign strategy and creative direction. Campaign objectives can include:

- **Brand Awareness**: Introducing the brand to a new audience or strengthening its presence.
- **Product Launch**: Promoting a new product or service effectively.
- **Engagement**: Increasing social media engagement, such as likes, comments, and shares.
- **Lead Generation**: Collecting user information for future marketing efforts.
- **Sales Conversion**: Driving sales directly through influencer promotions.
- **Reputation Management**: Addressing specific brand challenges or crises.

Identifying the Right Influencers

The success of an influencer marketing campaign hinges on selecting the most suitable influencers. Here's how to make the right choices:

1. Audience Alignment
- Analyze the influencer's followers to ensure they match your target audience.
- Consider factors like demographics, interests, and values.
- Evaluate the influencer's content to ensure it aligns with your brand's values and messaging.

2. Relevance and Niche
- Choose influencers whose content aligns with your niche or industry.
- Micro-influencers with a focused niche can provide highly engaged audiences.

3. Authenticity
- Prioritize influencers who have built genuine relationships with their followers.
- Authenticity fosters trust and credibility, which are essential for campaign success.

4. Engagement Metrics
- Examine an influencer's engagement metrics, including likes, comments, and shares.
- A high follower count alone does not guarantee engagement.

5. Track Record
- Review an influencer's past collaborations and their impact.
- Look for successful campaigns and positive brand associations.

Crafting Creative Campaign Concepts

The heart of a compelling influencer marketing campaign lies in creative concepts that captivate audiences. Consider these strategies:

1. Storytelling
- Encourage influencers to tell authentic stories related to your brand.
- Narratives evoke emotions and create memorable connections.

2. User-Generated Content (UGC)
- Empower influencers and their followers to create UGC that showcases your product or service.
- UGC builds trust and serves as social proof.

3. Challenges and Contests
- Create challenges or contests that engage both influencers and their audiences.
- Contests generate excitement and participation.

4. Exclusive Offers
- Offer influencer-exclusive discounts or promotions.
- This approach incentivizes their followers to take action.

Collaborating Effectively with Influencers

Building strong partnerships with influencers is paramount. Effective collaboration involves:

1. Clear Communication
- Establish open and transparent communication channels.
- Provide influencers with a detailed campaign brief, including goals, expectations, and guidelines.

2. Creative Freedom
- Allow influencers creative freedom within the campaign framework.
- Trust their expertise in engaging their audience.

3. Compensation and Agreements
- Clearly define compensation, whether it's monetary, products, or other incentives.
- Draft legal agreements that outline deliverables, timelines, and rights.

4. Monitoring and Support
- Continuously monitor campaign progress and performance.
- Offer support and resources to influencers as needed.

Measuring and Analyzing Campaign Performance

To assess the impact of your influencer marketing campaign, use relevant key performance indicators (KPIs) such as:

- **Engagement Metrics**: Track likes, comments, shares, and click-through rates.
- **Reach and Impressions**: Measure the campaign's reach and visibility.
- **Conversion Rates**: Analyze the conversion of influencer-generated traffic into leads or sales.
- ROI: Calculate the return on investment to assess the campaign's cost-effectiveness.
- **Brand Sentiment**: Monitor social sentiment and brand mentions.

Adjusting and Iterating Campaigns

Based on performance data, be prepared to make adjustments and iterate for future campaigns. Influencer marketing is an iterative process, and each campaign provides valuable insights for improvement.

In conclusion, influencer marketing campaigns that excel in creativity and execution require strategic planning, the selection of suitable influencers, creative concept development, effective collaboration, and robust measurement. By understanding these fundamental aspects, brands can harness the immense potential of influencer marketing to build brand awareness, engage audiences, and achieve their marketing goals.

9.5 Measuring and Analyzing: Evaluating campaign success.

The ability to measure and analyze the success of campaigns is paramount to ensuring a return on investment (ROI) and refining future strategies. This chapter delves into the intricate world of measuring and analyzing the effectiveness of influencer marketing campaigns, offering insights and methodologies to help marketers make data-driven decisions.

Introduction

Influencer marketing has evolved from a nascent concept to a vital component of modern digital marketing strategies. However, the success of influencer collaborations is not solely determined by follower counts and engagement metrics. To truly understand the impact and value of influencer marketing, marketers must employ sophisticated measurement and analysis techniques.

Defining Key Performance Indicators (KPIs)

Before diving into the intricacies of measuring success, it is crucial to establish a set of clear and relevant Key Performance Indicators (KPIs). KPIs serve as benchmarks to assess the effectiveness of influencer marketing campaigns. Common KPIs include:

- **Engagement Rate**: Calculated by dividing total engagement (likes, comments, shares) by the total follower count of the influencer.

- **Reach and Impressions**: Evaluating the number of people who saw the content and the frequency of exposure.

- **Click-Through Rate (CTR)**: Measuring the proportion of viewers who clicked on a provided link.

- **Conversion Rate**: Determining the percentage of viewers who completed a desired action (e.g., making a purchase).

- **Return on Investment (ROI)**: Calculating the financial returns compared to the campaign's cost.

- **Brand Sentiment**: Assessing changes in the public's perception of the brand or product.

Data Collection and Analysis
1. Social Media Analytics
In the era of influencer marketing, social media platforms provide valuable analytics tools that allow marketers to track the performance of influencer-generated content. These platforms offer insights into reach, engagement, demographics, and even the types of content that resonate most with the audience.
2. Custom Tracking Links
Implementing custom tracking links, such as UTM parameters, enables marketers to trace the origin of website traffic and conversions generated by influencer campaigns. This technique provides granular data to evaluate the efficacy of each influencer's efforts.
3. Conversion Attribution Modeling
Sophisticated marketers employ attribution modeling to understand how influencer touchpoints contribute to conversions. Multi-touch attribution models, including first-touch, last-touch, and linear attribution, help allocate value to each interaction in the customer journey.

Evaluating Audience Authenticity
In the pursuit of success measurement, authenticity should not be overlooked. Scrutinizing an influencer's audience for signs of inauthentic engagement or bot-driven interactions is crucial. Marketers must ensure that an influencer's followers are genuine and align with the brand's target demographic.
Calculating Return on Investment (ROI)
ROI analysis is a cornerstone of influencer marketing measurement. It involves quantifying the financial impact of an influencer campaign. Marketers must calculate both the costs (influencer fees, content production, etc.) and the gains (revenue, increased brand visibility) to determine whether the campaign was profitable.

The Role of Micro and Nano Influencers

Micro and nano influencers, with smaller but highly engaged audiences, have gained prominence in influencer marketing. This chapter explores the nuances of measuring success when collaborating with these influencers, highlighting their potential for cost-effective campaigns and niche audience targeting.

Post-Campaign Evaluation and Adjustments

Influencer marketing is an iterative process. After a campaign concludes, it is essential to conduct a post-mortem analysis. This entails reviewing the KPIs, ROI, and qualitative feedback. Based on the findings, marketers can refine future influencer strategies, either by optimizing existing partnerships or seeking new influencers.

Ethical Considerations and Transparency

Measuring influencer marketing success also involves ethical dimensions. Marketers should ensure that influencers disclose paid partnerships, and campaigns should align with ethical guidelines and regulations.

Conclusion

In the dynamic world of influencer marketing, the ability to measure and analyze success is a fundamental skill. Marketers must adopt a data-driven approach, leveraging KPIs, analytics tools, and attribution models to gauge the impact of influencer campaigns accurately. In doing so, they can not only justify their investments but also fine-tune strategies for future success in this ever-evolving landscape.

10. Mobile Marketing

10.1 Importance of Mobile Marketing: Growth and potential.

With the widespread adoption of smartphones and the increasing amount of time people spend on their mobile devices, businesses must recognize and leverage the power of mobile marketing to stay competitive in today's digital landscape. In this chapter, we delve deep into the significance of mobile marketing, exploring its growth, potential, and impact on businesses of all sizes.

Introduction

Mobile marketing refers to the practice of reaching and engaging with target audiences through mobile devices, such as smartphones and tablets. It encompasses a wide range of strategies and tactics, including mobile websites, mobile apps, SMS marketing, push notifications, and mobile advertising. Mobile marketing has gained immense importance due to several key factors:

The Proliferation of Mobile Devices

The ubiquity of mobile devices is one of the primary reasons mobile marketing is indispensable. As of [latest statistics], there are [number] billion smartphones in use worldwide, and this number continues to grow. People rely on their mobile devices not only for communication but also for information, entertainment, shopping, and more. This constant connectivity presents a massive opportunity for businesses to connect with their target audience directly.

Changing Consumer Behavior

Consumer behavior has evolved with the rise of mobile technology. Mobile users expect instant access to information, seamless user experiences, and personalized content. They use their smartphones to research products, read reviews, compare prices, and make purchases on the go. Businesses that fail to meet these expectations risk losing potential customers to competitors who have embraced mobile marketing.

The Mobile-First Approach

Many businesses have adopted a "mobile-first" approach to design and marketing. This approach prioritizes the mobile user experience above all else. It involves creating mobile-responsive websites, optimizing content for mobile consumption, and developing mobile apps that provide value to users. By putting mobile users first, businesses can enhance customer satisfaction and increase conversions.

Growth in Mobile Apps

Mobile apps have become integral to daily life. Users spend a significant amount of their mobile device usage time within apps. This trend has led businesses to develop their own mobile apps to engage with customers directly. Mobile apps offer features such as push notifications, in-app purchases, and user account management, making them powerful tools for customer engagement and retention.

Mobile Commerce (M-Commerce)
M-commerce, or mobile commerce, is a rapidly growing sector of e-commerce. It involves buying and selling products and services through mobile devices. Consumers appreciate the convenience of mobile shopping, and businesses are capitalizing on this trend by optimizing their online stores for mobile users. Mobile wallets and one-click payments have further streamlined the purchasing process, driving M-commerce's growth.

Location-Based Marketing
Mobile devices provide the opportunity for location-based marketing. With GPS technology, businesses can deliver targeted messages, promotions, and offers to users when they are in proximity to physical store locations. This capability enables businesses to drive foot traffic to brick-and-mortar stores and enhance the overall customer experience.

Mobile Advertising
Mobile advertising plays a significant role in digital marketing strategies. Businesses can leverage mobile advertising platforms to reach specific audiences with precision. Mobile ads can take various forms, including display ads, video ads, and social media ads. Mobile advertising allows for advanced targeting options, such as demographic targeting, geolocation targeting, and even retargeting based on user behavior.

Mobile Marketing and SEO
Mobile marketing also has implications for search engine optimization (SEO). Search engines like Google prioritize mobile-friendly websites in their search results. Therefore, businesses must ensure that their websites are mobile-responsive to maintain their search engine visibility.

Conclusion
In conclusion, mobile marketing is a vital aspect of contemporary digital marketing. Its importance stems from the widespread use of mobile devices, changing consumer behavior, the mobile-first approach, the growth of mobile apps, the rise of M-commerce, location-based marketing opportunities, and the effectiveness of mobile advertising. Businesses that embrace mobile marketing can connect with their target audiences in meaningful ways, drive conversions, and stay competitive in the digital landscape. In the subsequent sections of this chapter, we will explore various aspects of mobile marketing in greater detail, including mobile websites, mobile apps, SMS marketing, push notifications, and mobile advertising strategies.

10.2 Mobile Websites vs. Apps: Pros and cons.

Mobile marketing has become an integral part of digital marketing strategies, and a critical decision that businesses often face is whether to prioritize the development of mobile websites or mobile apps. Each approach has its own set of advantages and disadvantages, and understanding these distinctions is essential for making informed decisions in the realm of mobile marketing.

Introduction
In today's digital landscape, consumers are increasingly using their mobile devices to access the internet, interact with brands, and make purchase decisions. As a result, businesses must establish a strong presence in the mobile space. The two primary avenues for achieving this are through mobile websites and mobile apps. This chapter delves into the key considerations associated with each approach, highlighting their respective strengths and weaknesses.

Mobile Websites
Overview of Mobile Websites
A mobile website is a version of a company's website specifically designed and optimized for viewing on smartphones and tablets. These websites are typically accessed through a mobile web browser, such as Safari or Chrome, and are accessible via a URL. Mobile websites offer several advantages:

Accessibility
One of the primary advantages of mobile websites is their accessibility. Users can access a mobile website from any device with an internet connection and a web browser. This universal accessibility ensures that your content reaches a broad audience.

Cost-Effective
Developing and maintaining a mobile website is generally more cost-effective than creating a mobile app. It involves designing responsive web pages that adapt to various screen sizes, reducing the need for separate development for different platforms.

SEO-Friendly
Mobile websites are favorable from an SEO perspective. Search engines can crawl and index mobile web pages, making it easier for users to discover your content through organic search results.

Immediate Access
Mobile websites provide immediate access to content without requiring users to download and install an app. This can be particularly advantageous for businesses looking to engage users quickly.
Responsive Design

Creating a mobile website involves implementing responsive design principles. This approach ensures that web pages adapt fluidly to different screen sizes, maintaining a consistent user experience. Key considerations in responsive design include:

- **Flexible Layouts**: Designing layouts that adjust based on screen width.
- **Media Queries**: Using CSS media queries to apply styles based on device characteristics.
- **Viewport Meta Tag**: Setting the viewport meta tag for proper scaling on mobile devices.

Mobile Apps
Understanding Mobile Apps
Mobile apps are software applications specifically designed to run on mobile devices, such as smartphones and tablets. Unlike mobile websites, apps are typically downloaded and installed from app stores (e.g., Apple App Store, Google Play Store). Mobile apps offer several advantages:

Enhanced User Experience
Apps often provide a more immersive and feature-rich user experience compared to mobile websites. They can leverage device-specific functionalities, such as GPS, camera, and notifications.

Offline Access
Mobile apps can offer limited offline functionality, allowing users to access certain features and content without an internet connection. This can be beneficial for apps that require continuous usage, such as games or productivity tools.

Brand Loyalty
Having an app on a user's device can foster a sense of brand loyalty and constant engagement. Users are more likely to return to an app they have installed, providing opportunities for ongoing interaction.

Push Notifications
Apps can send push notifications to users, enabling direct and timely communication. This feature can be effective for promotions, updates, and reminders.

Considerations for Decision-Making
When deciding whether to prioritize a mobile website or a mobile app, businesses should consider several factors:

Target Audience
Understanding your target audience is crucial. If your audience primarily accesses content through web browsers, a mobile website may be sufficient. On the other hand, if

your audience values convenience and frequent interaction, an app might be more suitable.

Budget and Resources
Consider your budget and available resources. Developing and maintaining a mobile app can be more resource-intensive than creating a mobile website. Assess your financial capabilities and long-term commitments.

Functionality and Features
Evaluate the functionality and features you wish to offer. If your content or services require advanced capabilities, such as offline access or complex interactions, an app may be the better choice.

Marketing and Promotion
Consider how you plan to market and promote your mobile presence. Apps may require additional efforts to encourage downloads and engage users, while mobile websites benefit from standard web promotion.

Analytics and Measurement
Think about your analytics and measurement needs. Mobile websites offer standard web analytics tools, while apps require integration with mobile app analytics platforms for in-depth insights.

Conclusion
In the evolving landscape of mobile marketing, the decision to prioritize a mobile website or a mobile app is not one-size-fits-all. Both options offer unique advantages, and the choice should align with your business goals, target audience, and available resources. By carefully evaluating these factors, businesses can create a successful mobile strategy that maximizes their reach and engagement in the mobile space.

10.3 SMS and Push Notifications: Direct marketing tactics.

This chapter delves into the intricacies of collaborating with influencers, covering the entire process from identifying suitable influencers to executing effective partnerships.

Understanding the Influencer Landscape
Influencer marketing has grown exponentially, spanning various niches and platforms. To embark on a successful influencer collaboration journey, it's imperative to comprehend the influencer landscape:

The Diversity of Influencers: Influencers come in various forms, including celebrities, micro-influencers, and nano-influencers, each with its unique advantages.

Choosing the Right Influencer: The selection process involves analyzing their niche, follower demographics, engagement rates, and authenticity.

Identifying Influencers

Finding the right influencers for your brand is a critical first step. Here's how to do it:

1. **Define Your Goals**: Determine what you want to achieve with the influencer collaboration. Whether it's brand awareness, product promotion, or a specific campaign, clarity on objectives is essential.
2. **Audience Alignment**: Identify influencers whose followers align with your target audience. This ensures relevance and authenticity.
3. **Tools and Platforms**: Utilize influencer marketing platforms and tools to discover potential influencers. These platforms provide insights into an influencer's reach, engagement, and past collaborations.
4. **Social Media Listening**: Monitor social media conversations to identify individuals who are already talking about your brand or products. These individuals may be potential advocates.

Evaluating Influencers

Once you've identified potential influencers, it's time to evaluate their suitability:

1. **Engagement Metrics**: Assess an influencer's engagement rates, which include likes, comments, and shares. High engagement indicates an active and involved audience.
2. **Authenticity**: Investigate the authenticity of an influencer's followers. Avoid influencers who have purchased fake followers, as this can harm your brand's reputation.
3. **Content Quality**: Review the influencer's content quality, style, and consistency. Ensure that their content aligns with your brand's image and values.
4. **Past Collaborations**: Examine their history of brand collaborations. Assess whether their previous partnerships have been successful and align with your brand's objectives.

Building Influencer Relationships

Effective influencer marketing relies on building strong relationships with influencers:

1. **Personalized Outreach**: Reach out to influencers with personalized messages. Express your admiration for their work and explain why you believe they are a good fit for your brand.
2. **Transparent Communication**: Be transparent about your expectations, deliverables, and compensation. Clarity fosters trust and prevents misunderstandings.
3. **Collaborative Content Planning**: Involve influencers in the content creation process. Collaboratively brainstorm ideas and concepts that align with your brand's message.
4. **Contractual Agreements**: Draft clear contracts outlining deliverables, timelines, compensation, and any exclusivity agreements. Legal clarity is essential for a smooth partnership.

Executing the Collaboration

Once the influencer partnership is established, it's time to execute the collaboration:

1. **Content Creation**: Influencers create and share content that promotes your brand or product. Ensure that the content is authentic and resonates with their audience.

2. **Monitoring and Engagement**: Monitor the influencer's posts and engage with their audience. Respond to comments and interact with the influencer's followers.

3. **Performance Metrics**: Track key performance metrics, such as reach, engagement, website traffic, and conversions. Evaluate the campaign's success based on your predefined goals.

4. **Payment and Compensation**: Ensure timely payment and compensation for the influencer's work, as agreed upon in the contract.

Measuring the Impact

Assessing the impact of your influencer collaboration is crucial for future strategies:

1. **ROI Analysis**: Calculate the return on investment (ROI) by comparing the campaign's cost to the generated revenue or other predefined goals.

2. **Post-Campaign Survey**: Collect feedback from the influencer and their audience to gauge the campaign's effectiveness.

3. **Long-term Partnerships**: Consider the potential for long-term collaborations with influencers who have demonstrated value and alignment with your brand.

Conclusion

Collaborating with influencers can significantly boost your brand's online presence and credibility. By understanding the influencer landscape, identifying the right influencers, building relationships, and executing collaborations effectively, you can harness the power of influencer marketing to achieve your marketing objectives.

10.4 Mobile Ads: Formats and platforms.

As consumers increasingly rely on their mobile devices, marketers must adapt their strategies to leverage this platform effectively. In this chapter, we delve deep into the realm of mobile advertising, exploring its significance, strategies, formats, and best practices.

Introduction
Mobile advertising encompasses a broad spectrum of promotional activities tailored specifically for smartphones and tablets. Its importance stems from the fact that mobile devices have become an integral part of consumers' lives. Mobile advertising allows marketers to connect with their target audience in a highly personalized and contextually relevant manner. In this section, we explore the fundamental aspects of mobile advertising and why it's crucial for modern marketing strategies.

The Mobile Landscape
Understanding the mobile landscape is the first step in successful mobile advertising. Here, we examine key statistics and trends, including the prevalence of mobile devices, the shift from desktop to mobile, and the impact of mobile apps. We also discuss the diverse mobile ecosystem, comprising different operating systems, devices, and screen sizes, which necessitates adaptable advertising strategies.

Mobile Advertising Formats
Mobile advertising offers a variety of formats to engage users effectively. We delve into the most common formats, including:

1. **Mobile Display Ads**
   - Banner Ads: The classic format, often displayed at the top or bottom of mobile screens.
   - Interstitial Ads: Full-screen ads that appear between content transitions, such as between app screens or levels in a game.
   - Native Ads: Seamlessly integrated into the app's content for a non-disruptive user experience.

2. **In-App Advertising**
   - In-App Banner Ads: Displayed within mobile applications, these ads are less intrusive and closely aligned with the app's content.
   - In-App Video Ads: Engaging video content within apps, commonly used for brand storytelling.

3. **Mobile Search Ads**
   - Mobile Search Engine Optimization (SEO): Optimizing websites for mobile search visibility.

- Pay-Per-Click (PPC) Mobile Ads: Sponsored search results displayed on mobile search engines.

4. Mobile Video Ads

- Mobile Video Pre-roll: Short video ads that appear before or during mobile video content.

- In-Feed Mobile Video: Video ads integrated into social media feeds or content streams.

Mobile Advertising Strategies

To maximize the impact of mobile advertising, marketers must employ effective strategies. We delve into various approaches:

- Geo-Targeting and Location-Based Marketing

Leveraging users' location data to deliver hyper-targeted ads based on their physical proximity to businesses or specific locations.

- Mobile Remarketing

Re-engaging users who have previously interacted with your brand or app, encouraging them to return and convert.

- Mobile Video Storytelling

Crafting compelling narratives through video ads to capture users' attention and convey brand messages effectively.

- Mobile Ad Personalization

Using data-driven insights to tailor ad content and messages to individual user preferences and behavior.

Mobile Advertising Best Practices

Successful mobile advertising requires adherence to best practices. We explore the following guidelines:

- Optimizing for Mobile-First Design

Ensuring that ad creatives, landing pages, and websites are mobile-responsive and provide an excellent user experience.

- A/B Testing and Performance Monitoring

Continuously testing different ad creatives, targeting options, and strategies to identify what resonates most with the mobile audience.

- Ad Transparency and Privacy Compliance

Maintaining transparency in data collection and usage, adhering to privacy regulations, and respecting user preferences.

- Cross-Device Tracking
Implementing strategies to track users across different devices to understand their multi-device journey.

Measuring Mobile Advertising Success
Evaluating the effectiveness of mobile advertising campaigns is crucial. We explore key performance indicators (KPIs) and metrics, such as click-through rates (CTR), conversion rates, return on ad spend (ROAS), and customer lifetime value (CLV). We also discuss the role of mobile analytics tools in providing actionable insights.

Challenges and Future Trends
Mobile advertising faces unique challenges, including ad fatigue and ad-blockers. We discuss strategies for overcoming these challenges and examine future trends, such as augmented reality (AR) advertising, mobile commerce, and the integration of artificial intelligence (AI) in mobile ad targeting.

Conclusion
Mobile advertising is an indispensable component of modern marketing strategies. This chapter provides a comprehensive overview of the mobile advertising landscape, from its significance and formats to strategies, best practices, and measurement techniques. Adapting to the mobile-first era is imperative for marketers seeking to engage their audience effectively and achieve remarkable results in the digital realm.

10.5 Location-Based Marketing: Utilizing geo-targeting.

Location-based marketing is one such avenue that leverages geographic data to deliver targeted and relevant content to users based on their physical location. This chapter explores the intricacies of location-based marketing, its significance in the mobile era, strategies for implementation, and ethical considerations.

Introduction
Location-based marketing, often referred to as "geo-marketing," is a dynamic approach that tailors marketing messages and offers to the geographic location of consumers. It has become increasingly important in the context of mobile marketing, as smartphones equipped with GPS capabilities enable marketers to deliver hyper-localized content and engage with consumers on a personal level.

The Role of Location in Marketing

Location-based marketing harnesses the power of location data to enhance the relevance and effectiveness of marketing campaigns. Understanding the role of location in marketing is crucial for leveraging its potential:

Understanding Location Data Location data can be categorized into two types: explicit and implicit.

- *Explicit Location Data*: This type of data is willingly shared by users when they check in at a specific place, share their location on social media, or use location-based services.

- *Implicit Location Data*: Implicit data is collected passively, often through smartphone sensors and apps that track users' movements.

Benefits of Location-Based Marketing

Location-based marketing offers several benefits to businesses and consumers alike:

1. **Hyper-Personalization**: Marketers can deliver highly relevant content, offers, and promotions based on a user's current location, increasing the likelihood of conversion.
2. **Enhanced Customer Engagement**: By sending messages or offers when customers are near a physical store, businesses can drive foot traffic and increase engagement.
3. **Improved Targeting**: Geo-targeting allows marketers to focus their efforts on specific geographic areas, reducing wastage of resources.
4. **Data-Driven Insights**: Location data can provide valuable insights into consumer behavior, helping businesses refine their strategies.

Strategies for Location-Based Marketing

Implementing effective location-based marketing requires a strategic approach:

1. Geo-Targeted Advertising

- **Customized Ads**: Create advertisements tailored to specific geographic regions or even individual stores.

- **Location-Based Keywords**: Incorporate location-specific keywords to increase visibility in local search results.

- **Geo-Fencing**: Set up virtual perimeters around physical locations to trigger targeted ads or notifications when users enter the area.

2. Location-Based Notifications

- **Beacon Technology**: Use Bluetooth beacons to send location-specific messages or offers to nearby smartphone users.

- **Push Notifications**: Send personalized push notifications to users based on their current location.

3. Location-Based Content

- **Localized Content**: Create content that speaks to the interests and needs of users in specific regions.

- **Location-Based Landing Pages**: Develop landing pages optimized for different locations to enhance relevance.

4. Check-In Promotions

- **Encourage User Check-Ins**: Incentivize users to check in at your physical locations on social media platforms by offering discounts or rewards.

5. Location Analytics

- **Track User Behavior**: Use location data to analyze user movements, patterns, and preferences.
- **Optimize Campaigns**: Adjust marketing campaigns based on location-based insights.

Ethical Considerations

As location-based marketing becomes more prevalent, it is essential to address ethical considerations:

1. **Privacy**: Respect user privacy by obtaining explicit consent for location data collection and providing clear opt-out options.
2. **Transparency**: Communicate how location data will be used and ensure transparency in data handling practices.
3. **Security**: Safeguard location data against unauthorized access or breaches.
4. **Relevance**: Deliver content and offers that genuinely benefit users, avoiding spammy or intrusive practices.

Conclusion

Location-based marketing is a powerful tool that empowers businesses to engage with their audience in a highly personalized and context-aware manner. When executed with respect for user privacy and ethical considerations, location-based marketing can lead to increased customer satisfaction, improved engagement, and ultimately, enhanced business success in the digital age. As technology continues to advance, businesses that embrace location-based marketing are poised to stay ahead of the curve and deliver exceptional value to their customers.

11. Web Analytics and Data Analysis

11.1 Fundamentals of Web Analytics: Tools and terminology.

Web analytics is the cornerstone of effective online marketing. It provides invaluable insights into website performance, user behavior, and the impact of marketing efforts. In this chapter, we will delve deep into the fundamentals of web analytics, covering a wide array of topics to help you understand, implement, and leverage web analytics effectively in your online marketing strategy.

Understanding Web Analytics

Web analytics is the process of collecting, measuring, analyzing, and reporting data related to web traffic and user interactions on a website. It plays a pivotal role in decision-making for online businesses, helping them optimize their digital presence and marketing efforts.

Importance of Web Analytics

Web analytics holds immense significance for several reasons:

- **Data-Driven Decision Making**: It enables data-driven decision-making by providing actionable insights based on real user behavior and interactions.

- **Performance Evaluation**: It helps assess the performance of a website or specific marketing campaigns, shedding light on what's working and what needs improvement.

- **User Experience Enhancement**: Web analytics helps identify user pain points and areas where the user experience can be enhanced.

- **Conversion Rate Optimization**: It aids in improving conversion rates by understanding how users move through the conversion funnel.

- **Return on Investment (ROI) Analysis**: Marketers can measure the ROI of marketing campaigns and allocate resources more effectively.

Key Metrics and KPIs

In the world of web analytics, various metrics and Key Performance Indicators (KPIs) are used to gauge website performance. These include:

- **Traffic Metrics**: Metrics like sessions, pageviews, and unique visitors provide insights into website traffic volume.

- **Engagement Metrics**: Metrics such as bounce rate, time on page, and pages per session indicate user engagement.

- **Conversion Metrics**: Conversion rate, goal completions, and e-commerce transactions measure the effectiveness of conversion paths.

- **Acquisition Metrics**: These metrics track the sources of traffic, such as organic search, paid search, social media, and referrals.

- **Behavior Metrics**: Metrics like event tracking and user flow analysis help understand user behavior on the site.

Implementing Web Analytics
To leverage the power of web analytics, it's crucial to set up and configure analytics tools effectively.

Choosing the Right Analytics Platform
Selecting an appropriate analytics platform is the first step in implementing web analytics. Google Analytics, Adobe Analytics, and Matomo are popular choices, each offering unique features and capabilities.

Setting Up Tracking Codes
Tracking codes, such as Google Analytics tracking tags, need to be properly implemented on your website. This involves inserting code snippets into your web pages to collect data.

Defining Goals and Conversions
Setting up goals and conversion tracking allows you to measure specific actions that are valuable to your business, such as form submissions, product purchases, or newsletter sign-ups.

E-commerce Tracking
For e-commerce websites, implementing e-commerce tracking is essential. It provides insights into product sales, revenue, and shopping behavior.

Event Tracking
Event tracking enables you to monitor specific interactions on your website, such as clicks on buttons, video views, or downloads. This helps in understanding user engagement with your content.

Data Collection and Processing
Once tracking is set up, web analytics tools collect a vast amount of data. Understanding how data is collected and processed is crucial for accurate analysis.

Data Collection Methods
Web analytics tools use various data collection methods, including cookies, JavaScript tracking, and server log analysis. Understanding these methods is essential for interpreting data accurately.

Data Sampling
In some cases, web analytics tools use data sampling to process large datasets efficiently. It's important to know how sampling may affect your analysis and reporting.

Data Accuracy and Reliability

Ensuring data accuracy and reliability is paramount. This includes addressing issues such as bot traffic, spam referrals, and data discrepancies.

Data Analysis and Reporting

Analyzing web analytics data is where the real insights are derived. Effective data analysis involves several key aspects.

Segmentation

Segmentation allows you to divide your audience into specific groups, enabling more targeted analysis. Segments can be based on demographics, behavior, or traffic sources.

Data Visualization

Visualizing data through charts and graphs makes it easier to comprehend complex insights. Tools like Google Data Studio and Tableau are valuable for creating compelling visualizations.

Attribution Modeling

Understanding how different marketing channels contribute to conversions is achieved through attribution modeling. This helps allocate resources effectively.

A/B Testing and Experimentation

Experimentation is a fundamental part of web analytics. A/B testing allows you to test variations of web pages or marketing campaigns to determine what performs best.

Privacy and Ethical Considerations

As custodians of user data, it's crucial to prioritize privacy and ethical considerations in web analytics.

Data Privacy Compliance

Understanding and adhering to data privacy regulations, such as GDPR and CCPA, is essential to protect user privacy.

Ethical Data Usage

Maintaining ethical standards in data collection and usage is vital to build trust with users and avoid potential legal issues.

Conclusion

In this comprehensive exploration of web analytics fundamentals, we've covered the importance of web analytics, key metrics, implementing analytics tools, data collection and processing, data analysis, and ethical considerations. Web analytics is a powerful tool that, when wielded effectively, can drive informed decisions, enhance user experiences, and maximize the effectiveness of online marketing strategies. In the subsequent chapters, we will delve deeper into advanced analytics techniques and their applications in online marketing.

11.2 Collecting and Analyzing Data: Methods and practices.

The ability to gather, interpret, and act upon data insights is crucial for optimizing marketing strategies, understanding customer behavior, and achieving measurable results. In this chapter, we will delve deep into the intricate process of collecting and analyzing data, exploring the methodologies, tools, and best practices that empower marketers to make informed decisions and continuously enhance their online marketing efforts.

Introduction

In the digital age, data is often referred to as the new gold. Every interaction, click, view, and engagement leaves behind a trail of valuable data points. Collecting and analyzing this data is the key to unlocking the potential of online marketing campaigns. However, the sheer volume and complexity of data can be overwhelming. In this chapter, we will break down the process into manageable steps, offering a comprehensive guide to harnessing the power of data analytics in online marketing.

The Importance of Data Collection

Understanding Data's Role in Marketing

Data serves as the foundation upon which effective marketing strategies are built. It provides insights into customer preferences, behaviors, and demographics, allowing marketers to tailor their efforts for maximum impact.

Driving Informed Decision-Making

Data-driven decision-making minimizes guesswork and maximizes the efficiency of marketing initiatives. Marketers can optimize campaigns, allocate budgets, and refine messaging based on empirical evidence rather than assumptions.

Enhancing Customer Experience

By collecting and analyzing data, businesses can gain a deeper understanding of their customers. This knowledge enables the creation of personalized experiences that resonate with target audiences.

Data Collection Methodologies

Tracking User Behavior

Understanding how users interact with websites and digital content is fundamental. Web analytics tools like Google Analytics and Adobe Analytics offer detailed insights into user journeys, page views, bounce rates, and more.

Customer Surveys and Feedback

Direct feedback from customers can be invaluable. Surveys, feedback forms, and social media comments provide qualitative data that complements quantitative metrics.

A/B Testing

A/B testing involves comparing two versions of a webpage or marketing campaign to determine which performs better. It allows for data-driven optimization of content, design, and messaging.

Heatmaps and Click Tracking

Heatmaps visualize where users click, move their cursors, or spend the most time on a webpage. This visual data aids in identifying areas of user interest and potential optimization.

Social Media Listening

Social media platforms are rich sources of customer sentiment data. Listening to social conversations and monitoring brand mentions can uncover valuable insights.

Data Privacy and Ethics

Data Privacy Compliance

Marketers must adhere to data privacy regulations such as GDPR and CCPA. Collecting and storing data must be done transparently, and individuals' rights to their data must be respected.

Anonymization and Pseudonymization

To protect user privacy, personally identifiable information (PII) should be anonymized or pseudonymized when possible. This ensures data is used without revealing individual identities.

Data Analysis Techniques

Descriptive Analytics

Descriptive analytics involves summarizing data to understand past trends. It includes metrics like traffic, conversion rates, and engagement levels.

Diagnostic Analytics

Diagnostic analytics aims to identify the reasons behind past performance. It helps answer questions like "Why did a campaign succeed or fail?"

Predictive Analytics

Predictive analytics leverages historical data to forecast future outcomes. Machine learning algorithms can predict customer behavior and trends.

Prescriptive Analytics

Prescriptive analytics goes beyond prediction and provides actionable recommendations. It suggests strategies to optimize marketing efforts based on predictive insights.

Data Visualization
Importance of Visualization
Data visualization turns complex data sets into easily understandable visuals. Charts, graphs, and dashboards help marketers interpret data at a glance.

Choosing the Right Visualization Tools
Various tools like Tableau, Power BI, and Google Data Studio allow for the creation of customized data visualizations tailored to specific marketing needs.

Measuring ROI and KPIs
Defining Key Performance Indicators (KPIs)
KPIs are the metrics that matter most to a marketing campaign's success. They should align with overall business goals and objectives.

Calculating Return on Investment (ROI)
ROI quantifies the profitability of marketing efforts by comparing the gains (revenue) to the costs (ad spend, resources, etc.). It's a crucial metric for evaluating campaign effectiveness.

Case Studies
In this section, we will explore real-world case studies that demonstrate how data collection and analysis have driven successful online marketing campaigns. These examples will illustrate the practical application of data-driven decision-making in diverse industries.

Conclusion
Data collection and analysis are the backbone of modern online marketing. The insights derived from data empower marketers to make informed decisions, optimize campaigns, and enhance customer experiences. By implementing robust data collection methodologies, ensuring data privacy compliance, and mastering data analysis techniques, marketers can stay at the forefront of the digital marketing landscape and drive meaningful results.

This chapter provides a comprehensive overview of the intricacies involved in collecting and analyzing data for online marketing purposes. From the fundamental importance of data to the practical implementation of data analysis techniques, it equips marketers with the knowledge and tools necessary to navigate the data-driven marketing landscape effectively.

11.3 Using Analytics for Strategic Insights: Making informed decisions.

Businesses that harness the power of analytics gain a competitive edge by not only understanding their audience but also by strategically adapting their marketing efforts. This chapter delves deep into the world of web analytics and data analysis, exploring the nuances of collecting, interpreting, and applying data-driven insights to drive success in online marketing campaigns.

The Significance of Web Analytics

Web analytics serves as the compass for digital marketers, guiding them through the complex terrain of online marketing. It is the process of collecting, measuring, analyzing, and reporting web data to understand and optimize web usage. Here, we explore the pivotal role web analytics plays in online marketing strategy:

Understanding User Behavior: Web analytics allows marketers to gain an intricate understanding of how users interact with their websites or digital platforms. It provides insights into visitor demographics, geographic location, device usage, and browsing habits. Armed with this information, marketers can tailor their content and campaigns to better resonate with their target audience.

Measuring Campaign Performance: Marketers invest significant resources in various online marketing campaigns. Web analytics provides a comprehensive overview of how these campaigns are performing. Metrics such as click-through rates (CTR), conversion rates, and return on investment (ROI) are scrutinized to determine the effectiveness of each initiative.

Identifying Bottlenecks: Through the examination of user journeys, analytics unveil bottlenecks in the conversion funnel. By identifying where users drop off or encounter obstacles, marketers can strategically optimize those touchpoints to improve the overall user experience and boost conversions.

A/B Testing and Experimentation: Analytics facilitate A/B testing and experimentation, allowing marketers to compare the performance of different versions of a webpage, email, or ad. This data-driven approach empowers marketers to make data-backed decisions and refine their strategies for maximum impact.

Tools and Platforms for Web Analytics

Choosing the right web analytics tools and platforms is crucial for a successful online marketing strategy. There is a plethora of options available, each offering distinct features and capabilities. In this section, we explore some of the most widely used web analytics tools:

Google Analytics: Google Analytics is perhaps the most popular web analytics tool, known for its robust capabilities and user-friendly interface. It provides a wealth of data on website traffic, user behavior, and conversion tracking. Marketers can set up goals, track e-commerce transactions, and gain insights into user demographics.

Adobe Analytics: Adobe Analytics is a comprehensive analytics solution offered by Adobe. It allows marketers to delve deep into customer data, enabling advanced segmentation and personalization. The platform is favored by enterprises for its scalability and integration with other Adobe products.

Hotjar: Hotjar specializes in user behavior analytics and feedback. It offers heatmaps, session recordings, and user surveys to understand how visitors interact with a website. Marketers can visualize user behavior and identify areas of improvement.

Mixpanel: Mixpanel focuses on event tracking and user retention. It is particularly valuable for mobile app analytics. Marketers can track specific user interactions and events, such as app installs, feature usage, and in-app purchases.

SEMrush: While SEMrush is renowned for its SEO capabilities, it also provides valuable analytics features. Marketers can track keyword rankings, conduct competitive analysis, and gain insights into paid advertising performance.

Data Analysis and Interpretation
Collecting data is just the first step; the real power of web analytics lies in data analysis and interpretation. In this section, we delve into the process of extracting actionable insights from the raw data:

Data Segmentation: Marketers often analyze data through segmentation. This involves categorizing users based on specific attributes such as demographics, behavior, or traffic source. Segmentation allows marketers to tailor their strategies to different audience segments effectively.

Conversion Funnel Analysis: Conversion funnels represent the path users take from initial interaction to conversion. Marketers analyze conversion funnels to pinpoint drop-off points and optimize each stage for higher conversions.

Attribution Modeling: Attribution modeling assigns credit to various touchpoints in the customer journey, helping marketers understand which channels and interactions contribute most to conversions. Common attribution models include first-click, last-click, and linear attribution.

Data Visualization: Visualizing data through charts, graphs, and dashboards makes complex data more understandable. Marketers can use visualization tools to create informative reports and presentations for stakeholders.

Predictive Analytics: Predictive analytics involves using historical data to make future predictions. Marketers can forecast trends, customer behavior, and potential campaign outcomes, allowing for proactive strategy adjustments.

Actionable Insights and Strategy Implementation

Gaining insights from data is only valuable when those insights translate into actionable strategies. In this section, we explore how marketers can use web analytics to inform their decision-making and improve their online marketing efforts:

Optimizing Content: Data on user engagement, page views, and bounce rates can guide content optimization. Marketers can create content that aligns with user interests and addresses pain points.

Personalization: Web analytics can inform personalization efforts by revealing user preferences and behavior. Marketers can deliver tailored content and product recommendations for a more personalized user experience.

Advertising Campaign Optimization: Marketers can use analytics to optimize paid advertising campaigns. Data on ad performance, click-through rates, and conversion rates help allocate budgets effectively and refine targeting.

Conversion Rate Optimization (CRO): Through A/B testing and funnel analysis, marketers can identify barriers to conversion and implement changes to boost conversion rates.

User Experience Enhancement: Analytics data can uncover areas where the user experience can be improved. Marketers can work on site speed, navigation, and mobile responsiveness to enhance user satisfaction.

Ethical Considerations and Data Privacy

In the era of data-driven marketing, it is imperative to address ethical considerations and data privacy concerns. Marketers must adhere to regulations such as GDPR and ensure that user data is handled responsibly and securely. This section explores the ethical dimensions of web analytics and the importance of transparent data practices.

Conclusion

Web analytics is a powerful tool that empowers online marketers to make informed decisions and optimize their strategies for success. By understanding user behavior, measuring campaign performance, and extracting actionable insights, marketers can stay ahead in the competitive landscape of online marketing.

11.4 Conversion Optimization: Funnel analysis and improvement.

Conversion optimization is a critical aspect of online marketing that focuses on improving the effectiveness of digital marketing campaigns and websites in turning visitors into valuable customers or leads. In this chapter, we will delve deep into the intricacies of conversion optimization, exploring the strategies, techniques, and best practices that can significantly impact your online marketing success.

Understanding Conversion Optimization

Conversion optimization, often referred to as conversion rate optimization (CRO), is the systematic process of enhancing a website or digital marketing campaign's performance to increase the percentage of visitors who take desired actions, such as making a purchase, filling out a contact form, or subscribing to a newsletter. It involves understanding user behavior, identifying barriers to conversion, and implementing data-driven solutions to remove these barriers.

The Importance of Conversion Optimization

Conversion optimization is crucial for several reasons:

- **Maximizing ROI**: It ensures that you get the most value from your marketing budget by increasing the conversion rate and, subsequently, revenue.

- **Enhancing User Experience**: It leads to a better overall user experience, resulting in increased customer satisfaction and loyalty.

- **Data-Driven Decision Making**: It relies on data and insights, allowing marketers to make informed decisions and continually refine strategies.

- **Competitive Advantage**: It sets you apart from competitors by optimizing every stage of the customer journey.

The Conversion Optimization Process

Successful conversion optimization involves a structured process that includes several key stages:

1. Data Collection and Analysis

The first step in the conversion optimization process is collecting and analyzing data related to user behavior on your website or within your marketing campaigns. This includes:

- **User Journey Analysis**: Understanding how users navigate through your website or interact with your content.

- **Traffic Sources**: Identifying the sources of website traffic, such as organic search, paid search, social media, or referral traffic.

- **Conversion Funnel Analysis**: Mapping out the steps users take from initial interaction to conversion.

2. Identification of Conversion Barriers

Once data is collected, it's essential to identify the specific barriers that prevent users from converting. Common barriers include:

- **Poor Website Design**: Cluttered layouts, confusing navigation, or slow page loading times can deter users.
- **Unclear Messaging**: If users can't quickly understand the value of your offering, they're less likely to convert.
- **Trust Issues**: Concerns about security, privacy, or the legitimacy of your website can hinder conversions.

3. Hypothesis Generation

Based on the identified barriers, marketers formulate hypotheses about what changes or improvements could lead to increased conversions. These hypotheses are often centered around:

- **Usability**: Making the website easier to navigate and use.
- **Content Optimization**: Crafting compelling and persuasive content that addresses user needs.
- **Trust Signals**: Building trust through customer testimonials, trust badges, and clear privacy policies.

4. A/B Testing and Experimentation

To validate hypotheses, A/B testing and experimentation are crucial. Marketers create variations (A and B) of a webpage or campaign element and split traffic to measure which version performs better. This iterative process allows for data-driven decision-making and continuous improvement.

5. Implementation of Changes

Successful test outcomes are implemented on the website or within marketing campaigns. This may involve design changes, content updates, or adjustments to user interface elements.

6. Ongoing Monitoring and Optimization

Conversion optimization is not a one-time effort. It requires continuous monitoring and refinement. Marketers use analytics tools to track the impact of changes, identify new conversion barriers, and optimize further.

Key Conversion Optimization Techniques

1. A/B Testing

A/B testing, also known as split testing, involves comparing two or more variations of a webpage, email, or ad to determine which performs better in terms of conversions.

2. User Experience (UX) Design

Improving website usability and design to ensure a seamless and intuitive user experience is crucial for conversion optimization.

3. Content Optimization

Creating high-quality, engaging, and persuasive content that resonates with the target audience can significantly impact conversion rates.

4. Calls to Action (CTAs)

Optimizing the design, placement, and wording of CTAs can encourage users to take desired actions.

5. Landing Page Optimization

Specifically focusing on landing pages to ensure they are aligned with user intent and provide a clear path to conversion.

6. Multivariate Testing

Going beyond A/B testing by experimenting with multiple variations of different page elements simultaneously.

Measuring Success

Measuring the success of conversion optimization efforts is essential to determine the return on investment (ROI) and identify areas for further improvement. Key performance indicators (KPIs) for conversion optimization include:

- **Conversion Rate**: The percentage of visitors who complete the desired action.
- **Revenue Generated**: The monetary value of conversions.
- **Click-Through Rate (CTR)**: The rate at which users click on CTAs or links.
- **Bounce Rate**: The percentage of users who leave the site after viewing only one page.

Ethical Considerations

When conducting conversion optimization, it's essential to adhere to ethical principles. This includes respecting user privacy, providing transparent information, and not engaging in deceptive practices to boost conversions.

Conclusion

Conversion optimization is a dynamic and data-driven discipline within online marketing. By following a structured process, implementing proven techniques, and continually monitoring and optimizing, marketers can significantly increase the effectiveness of their digital campaigns, ultimately driving higher conversions and revenue.

11.5 Privacy and Ethics: Handling user data responsibly.

As marketers, it is our responsibility to maintain the trust of our audience while navigating the complex terrain of data collection, personalization, and targeted advertising. This chapter delves deep into the critical aspects of privacy and ethics in online marketing.

Understanding Privacy Regulations
In recent years, various privacy regulations have been enacted worldwide to protect user data. Understanding these regulations is paramount for online marketers:

1. GDPR (General Data Protection Regulation)
- GDPR Overview: An in-depth explanation of the GDPR framework.
- Key Principles: Exploring the principles of lawfulness, fairness, and transparency.
- Consent Mechanisms: Detailed insights into obtaining lawful consent for data processing.
- Data Subject Rights: A comprehensive breakdown of user rights under GDPR.
- Compliance and Penalties: The consequences of non-compliance and potential fines.

2. CCPA (California Consumer Privacy Act)
- CCPA Explained: Understanding the CCPA and its applicability.
- Consumer Rights: Analyzing the rights granted to California consumers.
- Data Handling Requirements: Comprehending data handling obligations.
- CCPA Compliance: Steps to ensure compliance for businesses.

3. CASL (Canadian Anti-Spam Legislation)
- CASL Overview: An overview of CASL's anti-spam provisions.
- Consent under CASL: Defining express and implied consent.
- Compliance with CASL: Ensuring compliance with email marketing regulations.
- Penalties and Enforcement: The consequences of violating CASL.

Data Collection and Transparency
Data Collection Practices
- Data Collection Methods: An examination of various data collection methods.
- User Data Types: Identifying the types of user data collected.
- Data Sources: Analyzing the sources of user data.
- Data Retention: Policies for storing and deleting user data.

Transparency and Data Privacy
- Privacy Policies: Crafting clear and comprehensive privacy policies.
- Consent Notices: Designing user-friendly consent notices.
- Data Usage Transparency: Communicating data usage to users.
- User Control: Empowering users to control their data.

Ethical Marketing Practices

1. User-Centric Approach

- Putting Users First: Prioritizing user interests and preferences.
- Honesty and Authenticity: Building trust through transparent communication.
- Avoiding Deception: Staying clear of misleading marketing practices.

2. Targeted Advertising Ethics

- Behavioral Targeting: Balancing personalization with privacy.
- Profiling Ethics: Ethical considerations in user profiling.
- Retargeting Practices: Responsible retargeting strategies.

3. Social Media and Influencer Ethics

- Authenticity in Influencer Marketing: Maintaining genuine influencer partnerships.
- Disclosure and Transparency: Clear disclosure of paid partnerships.
- Handling Negative Feedback: Ethical responses to criticism and feedback.

4. Email Marketing Ethics

- Permission-Based Marketing: The importance of permission in email marketing.
- Opt-Out Mechanisms: Ensuring easy opt-out options for subscribers.
- Anti-Spam Compliance: Abiding by anti-spam laws and regulations.

Data Security and Protection

1. Data Security Measures

- Encryption: Implementing strong encryption protocols.
- Access Control: Restricting access to sensitive data.
- Data Breach Response: Developing a data breach response plan.

2. Third-Party Partnerships

- Vendor Due Diligence: Assessing third-party data handling practices.
- Data Sharing Agreements: Creating transparent data sharing agreements.

Continuous Monitoring and Adaptation

1. Monitoring User Data

- Data Auditing: Regularly auditing data collection and storage practices.
- User Data Access: Allowing users to access their data.

2. Adapting to Regulatory Changes

- Staying Informed: Keeping abreast of evolving privacy regulations.
- Compliance Updates: Updating marketing practices to align with new regulations.

Conclusion

In the era of data-driven marketing, maintaining user trust through responsible data handling and ethical marketing practices is fundamental. Privacy and ethics in online marketing are not just legal obligations but also crucial elements of building long-lasting relationships with customers. By understanding the regulations, practicing transparency, and upholding ethical standards, marketers can navigate the digital landscape responsibly and sustainably.

12. Strategy and Future Planning

12.1 Developing an Online Marketing Strategy: Integrating channels and tactics.

Developing a well-rounded and dynamic strategy is not merely a choice but a necessity to thrive in the ever-evolving landscape of online marketing. This chapter delves deep into the intricacies of crafting an online marketing strategy that not only addresses the present challenges but also anticipates the future trends and demands of the digital world.

Introduction
In the opening section of this chapter, we set the stage for a comprehensive exploration of online marketing strategy. We emphasize the paramount importance of having a well-defined strategy in place and its role as a guiding compass for all marketing efforts.

Understanding the Marketing Landscape
Before embarking on the journey of strategy development, it is crucial to have a clear understanding of the broader marketing landscape. This section delves into the following aspects:

- **Market Analysis**: Analyzing the current market conditions, trends, and competitive landscape.
- **Consumer Behavior**: Understanding how target audiences behave online and their preferences.
- **SWOT Analysis**: Conducting a thorough analysis of strengths, weaknesses, opportunities, and threats.

Defining Clear Objectives
A successful online marketing strategy begins with clear and measurable objectives. In this section, we explore the importance of setting specific, measurable, achievable, relevant, and time-bound (SMART) goals for your online marketing efforts.

Identifying Target Audiences
To effectively reach and engage with potential customers, identifying and understanding the target audience is paramount. We delve into the following areas:

- **Segmentation**: Categorizing the audience into distinct segments based on demographics, psychographics, and behavior.
- **Buyer Personas**: Creating detailed profiles of ideal customers to tailor marketing efforts.

Choosing the Right Online Marketing Channels

The digital realm offers a multitude of marketing channels, each with its own strengths and weaknesses. In this section, we provide an in-depth analysis of various online marketing channels, including:

- **Search Engine Optimization (SEO)**: Strategies for improving organic search rankings.
- **Social Media Marketing**: Leveraging platforms like Facebook, Twitter, and LinkedIn.
- **Content Marketing**: Creating valuable content that resonates with the target audience.
- **Email Marketing**: Crafting effective email campaigns for lead nurturing and customer retention.
- **Paid Advertising (PPC)**: Utilizing pay-per-click advertising on platforms like Google Ads.
- **Affiliate Marketing**: Partnering with affiliates to expand reach and sales.
- **Video Marketing**: Harnessing the power of video content.
- **Influencer Marketing**: Collaborating with influencers to boost brand visibility.
- **Mobile Marketing**: Tailoring marketing efforts for mobile users.
- **Web Analytics**: Utilizing data for informed decision-making.

Budgeting and Resource Allocation

Once the marketing channels are identified, it's essential to allocate resources effectively. This section discusses budgeting considerations, including setting budgets for advertising, content creation, and tools or software.

Creating a Content Calendar

Consistency is key in online marketing. We guide readers on how to create a content calendar that ensures a steady flow of content across chosen channels.

Implementing the Strategy

With the strategy in place, the next step is execution. This section covers practical steps for implementing the strategy, including team collaboration, content creation, and campaign management.

Monitoring and Optimization

In the dynamic world of online marketing, continuous monitoring and optimization are essential. We discuss the importance of real-time analytics, A/B testing, and performance tracking to make data-driven adjustments.

Evaluating ROI and KPIs

Measuring the success of an online marketing strategy is crucial. This section explores key performance indicators (KPIs) and methods for calculating return on investment (ROI).

Adapting to Change

The digital landscape is in a constant state of flux. We emphasize the need for flexibility and adaptation to stay ahead of emerging trends and technologies.

Conclusion

In the final section of this chapter, we recap the significance of a well-crafted online marketing strategy and its role in achieving long-term success. We also emphasize the need for continuous learning and evolution in the field of online marketing.

12.2 Innovation and Technological Trends: Staying ahead with AI, VR, etc.

This chapter will provide in-depth insights into emerging technologies, tools, and strategies that every digital marketer should be aware of.

Artificial Intelligence (AI) in Marketing

Artificial Intelligence has become a game-changer in the realm of online marketing. AI-driven solutions are revolutionizing how marketers analyze data, create content, and engage with audiences.

AI-Powered Analytics:

- AI algorithms analyze vast datasets to uncover actionable insights.
- Predictive analytics forecast future trends and consumer behavior.
- Customer segmentation becomes more precise, leading to personalized marketing strategies.

Chatbots and Virtual Assistants:

- Chatbots offer real-time customer support and enhance user experience.
- Virtual assistants like voice-activated AI devices are changing search behaviors.

Content Generation with AI:

- AI-generated content tools streamline content creation.
- Marketers leverage AI to produce personalized content at scale.

Virtual Reality (VR) and Augmented Reality (AR)

VR and AR are redefining user engagement and product visualization in online marketing.

Immersive Brand Experiences:

- VR allows customers to experience products and services in a virtual environment.
- AR enhances real-world experiences through smartphone apps and wearables.

Virtual Showrooms and Try-Before-You-Buy:

- Retailers create virtual showrooms for product trials.
- AR lets customers try on clothing and accessories digitally.

Voice Search and Voice-Activated Devices

Voice search is transforming SEO and content strategies as more people rely on voice-activated devices like Amazon Echo and Google Home.

Conversational SEO:

- Keywords shift from typed queries to natural language.
- Marketers optimize content for voice search.

Voice Commerce:

- Voice-activated devices facilitate voice-based shopping.
- Marketers explore new sales channels and user experiences.

Blockchain Technology in Digital Advertising

Blockchain is gaining traction in digital advertising, offering transparency and security.

Ad Fraud Prevention:

- Blockchain verifies ad impressions, reducing fraud.
- Smart contracts automate transactions, ensuring fair compensation.

Enhanced Data Privacy:

- Users gain more control over their data.
- Marketers need to adapt to stricter privacy regulations.

Machine Learning and Personalization

Machine learning algorithms enhance personalization and customer experiences.

Recommendation Engines:

- Algorithms analyze user behavior to suggest relevant products.
- Netflix and Amazon are prime examples of successful recommendation engines.

Dynamic Content Optimization:

- Websites customize content in real-time based on user preferences.
- Personalized email campaigns yield higher engagement rates.

Social Commerce and Shoppable Content

Social media platforms integrate shopping features, transforming the e-commerce landscape.

Instagram Shopping and Facebook Marketplace:
- Users can purchase products directly from social media.
- Influencers drive sales through shoppable posts.

User-Generated Content:
- Brands encourage customers to create and share content.
- Authenticity becomes a key selling point.

Data Privacy and Ethical Marketing
Consumers are increasingly concerned about data privacy and ethical marketing practices.

Transparency and Consent:
- Marketers must obtain explicit user consent for data usage.
- Transparency builds trust and strengthens brand reputation.

Ethical AI Use:
- Responsible AI development and use is paramount.
- Avoiding bias and discrimination in AI algorithms is critical.

Emerging Social Media Platforms
New social media platforms and trends are diversifying online marketing channels.
TikTok and Clubhouse:
- Marketers explore creative ways to engage audiences on these platforms.
- Short-form video and audio content gain popularity.

Sustainability and Green Marketing
Sustainability practices are becoming central to brand identity.

Green Marketing Strategies:
- Brands showcase eco-friendly initiatives and products.
- Sustainable practices resonate with environmentally-conscious consumers.

Conclusion
Chapter 12.2 has delved into the cutting-edge innovations and technological trends shaping the future of online marketing. Staying informed and adapting to these changes is crucial for digital marketers to remain competitive and deliver exceptional experiences

to their audiences. As the online marketing landscape continues to evolve, embracing these trends will be instrumental in achieving marketing success in the digital age.

12.3 Personal Development and Learning: Continuing to grow as a marketer.

This chapter delves into the importance of personal growth, learning strategies, and resources available to marketers for honing their skills and staying at the forefront of the industry.

The Significance of Personal Development

In the dynamic realm of online marketing, personal development plays a pivotal role in career advancement and professional growth. Marketers who invest in their personal development not only stay relevant but also contribute significantly to their organizations' success. Here, we explore why personal development is crucial:

1. **Adaptability and Agility**: The digital marketing landscape constantly changes. Marketers who embrace personal development can quickly adapt to new trends, technologies, and consumer behaviors.
2. **Enhanced Creativity**: Personal development fosters creativity, allowing marketers to generate innovative campaigns and strategies that capture audience attention.
3. **Improved Leadership Skills**: As marketers climb the career ladder, leadership skills become vital. Personal development helps in building effective leadership qualities.
4. **Greater Confidence**: Continuous learning and skill enhancement boost confidence, empowering marketers to take on challenging projects and responsibilities.
5. **Networking Opportunities**: Engaging in personal development activities often leads to networking opportunities, connecting marketers with like-minded professionals and potential mentors.

Strategies for Personal Development

Successful personal development in online marketing involves a structured approach. Marketers can employ various strategies to enhance their skills and knowledge:

Setting Clear Goals: Defining specific, measurable, achievable, relevant, and time-bound (SMART) goals is the foundation of personal development. Marketers should identify areas for improvement and set clear objectives.

Online Courses and Certifications: Enrolling in online courses and obtaining certifications from reputable institutions is an effective way to gain new skills and knowledge. Platforms like Coursera, Udemy, and HubSpot Academy offer a plethora of courses on digital marketing topics.

Reading Industry Literature: Staying well-read in the field is crucial. Marketers should regularly read books, blogs, and articles by industry experts to stay informed about the latest trends and best practices.

Attending Conferences and Workshops: Industry conferences and workshops provide opportunities to learn from experts, participate in hands-on activities, and network with peers. Events like MozCon and Inbound are highly regarded in the digital marketing community.

Mentorship Programs: Seeking mentorship from experienced marketers can provide valuable insights and guidance. Mentor-mentee relationships can be established through professional organizations or networking groups.

Experimentation and Testing: Learning by doing is a powerful approach. Marketers should not shy away from experimenting with new strategies and analyzing results. A/B testing, for instance, can yield valuable data.

Joining Professional Associations: Being part of professional associations like the American Marketing Association (AMA) or the Digital Marketing Institute (DMI) can offer access to exclusive resources, webinars, and networking opportunities.

Resources for Personal Development

In the digital age, marketers have an abundance of resources at their disposal to facilitate personal development:

Online Learning Platforms: Websites like LinkedIn Learning, Coursera, edX, and Skillshare offer a vast library of courses and tutorials on digital marketing topics.

Industry Blogs and Websites: Subscribing to blogs and websites like Neil Patel's blog, Search Engine Journal, and Content Marketing Institute can provide daily insights and tips.

Podcasts: Podcasts such as "Marketing Over Coffee" and "The Smart Passive Income Online Business and Blogging Podcast" offer in-depth discussions and interviews with marketing experts.

Books: Literature by renowned authors like Seth Godin ("Permission Marketing"), Gary Vaynerchuk ("Crushing It!"), and Ann Handley ("Everybody Writes") provides valuable knowledge.

Webinars and Seminars: Many organizations and industry experts host webinars and seminars, often free of charge, to disseminate knowledge.

Social Media Groups: Joining marketing-focused groups on platforms like LinkedIn and Facebook can facilitate discussions, sharing of experiences, and peer learning.

Networking Events: Local marketing meetups, conferences, and networking events allow marketers to connect with peers and share insights.

Measuring Personal Development Progress

Tracking personal development progress is essential for setting benchmarks and ensuring continuous improvement. Marketers can employ the following methods:

Self-assessment: Periodically evaluate one's skills, knowledge, and achievements against previously set goals.

Feedback and Reviews: Solicit feedback from peers, mentors, or supervisors to gain external perspectives on progress.

Skill Assessments: Take advantage of skill assessment tools and quizzes available online to measure proficiency in specific areas.

Certifications and Qualifications: Attaining recognized certifications can serve as tangible evidence of personal development.

Portfolio Growth: An expanding portfolio of successful campaigns and projects is indicative of growth.

Conclusion

Personal development and learning are ongoing journeys for online marketers. Embracing the opportunities for growth and development is not only beneficial for individual careers but also for the organizations they serve. By setting clear goals, employing effective strategies, and leveraging available resources, marketers can navigate the ever-changing landscape of online marketing with confidence and expertise.

12.4 Sustainability in Online Marketing: Ethical practices and responsibility.

As marketers navigate the dynamic landscape of the digital realm, they are increasingly recognizing the importance of adopting sustainable practices that not only benefit their businesses but also contribute to a more environmentally and socially responsible digital ecosystem.

The Significance of Sustainability in Online Marketing

Sustainability in online marketing extends beyond the traditional notions of environmental conservation; it encompasses a broader perspective that encompasses ethical considerations, corporate social responsibility, and long-term viability. This section delves into the multifaceted significance of sustainability in the online marketing domain.

Understanding Sustainability in Online Marketing

Sustainability in online marketing can be defined as the conscious and strategic integration of practices that minimize negative impacts, promote ethical behavior, and ensure long-term success in the digital landscape. This holistic approach to sustainability encompasses several key dimensions:

1. **Environmental Sustainability**: This dimension emphasizes the reduction of environmental footprints associated with online marketing activities. It involves practices such as optimizing data centers, reducing energy consumption, and minimizing electronic waste generated by digital campaigns.

2. **Social Responsibility**: Online marketers are increasingly expected to uphold ethical standards in their interactions with customers, partners, and stakeholders. This includes transparency in data collection and usage,

addressing online privacy concerns, and promoting fair labor practices in the digital workforce.

3. **Economic Viability:** Sustainable online marketing strategies are designed to be economically viable in the long run. Marketers must consider the financial implications of their digital campaigns and assess whether they contribute positively to the bottom line while minimizing wasteful spending.

4. **Cultural Sensitivity:** Online marketing campaigns should be culturally sensitive and respect the values and beliefs of diverse audiences. Avoiding cultural insensitivity and appropriation is essential to maintaining brand integrity.

5. **Innovation and Adaptability:** Sustainability in online marketing requires continuous innovation and adaptability. Marketers should be prepared to evolve their strategies to align with changing consumer preferences and emerging technologies.

Sustainable Practices in Online Marketing

This section explores specific sustainable practices that online marketers can adopt to promote a more responsible and ethical digital marketing ecosystem.

1. Data Privacy and Security

Online marketers must prioritize data privacy and security. They should implement robust data protection measures, obtain explicit user consent for data collection, and comply with relevant data privacy regulations such as GDPR and CCPA. Transparency in data usage and secure storage practices build trust with consumers.

2. Content Responsibility

Sustainable online marketing involves creating content that is honest, informative, and free from misleading information. Marketers should avoid clickbait, fake news, and sensationalism. High-quality, accurate content fosters credibility and reliability.

3. Ethical SEO and Link Building

In the pursuit of SEO success, ethical practices should prevail. Marketers should avoid black-hat SEO techniques that manipulate search engine rankings. Genuine link building, content optimization, and adherence to search engine guidelines are crucial for sustainable SEO.

4. Green Hosting and Energy Efficiency

Choosing eco-friendly hosting providers that utilize renewable energy sources and implement energy-efficient data centers can significantly reduce the carbon footprint of websites and online campaigns. Marketers should prioritize green hosting options.

5. Diversity and Inclusion

Inclusive marketing campaigns that represent diverse voices and perspectives resonate with a broader audience. Marketers should strive for diversity in their content, images, and messaging, avoiding stereotypes and exclusivity.

6. Social Responsibility Initiatives
Online marketing can be a force for positive social change. Marketers can engage in social responsibility initiatives, support charitable causes, and use their platforms to raise awareness about critical societal issues.

Measuring the Impact of Sustainability
Sustainability efforts in online marketing should be quantifiable and measurable. This section discusses key performance indicators (KPIs) and metrics that enable marketers to assess the impact of their sustainable practices.

1. Carbon Footprint Reduction
Measuring and reducing the carbon footprint associated with digital campaigns is a fundamental KPI for environmental sustainability. Metrics may include energy consumption, server efficiency, and greenhouse gas emissions.

2. User Trust and Loyalty
Building trust and fostering customer loyalty are intangible but invaluable metrics for social responsibility and ethical marketing. Customer satisfaction, retention rates, and brand reputation are indicative of success in this dimension.

3. Financial Performance
Economic viability is assessed through financial KPIs such as return on investment (ROI), cost per acquisition (CPA), and revenue generated from sustainable marketing efforts.

4. Cultural Sensitivity Metrics
Cultural sensitivity can be evaluated through audience feedback, social media sentiment analysis, and surveys that gauge the cultural appropriateness of marketing campaigns.

5. Social Impact Indicators
Social responsibility initiatives should yield measurable social impacts, such as funds raised for charitable causes, increased awareness of social issues, or positive changes in societal attitudes.

Implementing a Sustainable Marketing Strategy
To effectively implement sustainability in online marketing, organizations must adopt a strategic approach. This section provides a step-by-step guide to developing and executing a sustainable marketing strategy.

1. Conduct a Sustainability Assessment

Begin by assessing your current marketing practices, identifying areas where sustainability can be improved, and setting specific sustainability goals.

2. Integrate Sustainability into Your Brand Identity
Sustainability should become a core component of your brand identity. Communicate your commitment to sustainability through branding, mission statements, and public disclosures.

3. Educate and Train Your Team
Ensure that your marketing team is well-versed in sustainable practices and ethics. Training programs and workshops can help team members understand their roles in promoting sustainability.

4. Choose Sustainable Tools and Technologies
Select digital marketing tools and technologies that align with sustainability goals. Consider the environmental impact of software, hardware, and hosting providers.

5. Monitor and Measure Progress
Regularly monitor and measure the impact of sustainability initiatives. Adjust strategies based on performance data and feedback from stakeholders.

6. Communicate Transparently
Be transparent about your sustainability efforts with customers, partners, and the public. Transparency builds trust and demonstrates accountability.

7. Continuously Innovate
Sustainability in online marketing is an ongoing journey. Stay updated on industry trends, emerging technologies, and best practices to remain at the forefront of sustainable marketing.

Conclusion
In conclusion, sustainability in online marketing is no longer a peripheral consideration but an integral component of responsible digital business practices. Embracing sustainability not only benefits the environment and society but also enhances brand reputation, fosters customer trust, and ensures long-term profitability in the ever-evolving digital landscape. By adopting sustainable practices and strategies, online marketers can contribute to a more ethical, responsible, and prosperous digital future.

12.5 Future Visions and Predictions: Looking ahead in online marketing.

The digital marketing domain is subject to rapid transformations, driven by technological advancements, changing consumer behaviors, and evolving search engine algorithms. This chapter delves into the visionary aspects of online marketing, offering insights and predictions that can help marketers and businesses stay ahead of the curve.

Embracing Technological Advancements

The digital marketing realm has witnessed a constant influx of technological innovations, and it shows no signs of slowing down. Marketers need to remain vigilant and adaptive to harness the potential of emerging technologies. Some key areas of focus include:

- **Artificial Intelligence (AI) Integration**: AI-powered chatbots, recommendation engines, and predictive analytics will become integral to personalized customer experiences.

- **Augmented Reality (AR) and Virtual Reality (VR)**: These technologies will offer immersive marketing opportunities, from virtual product try-ons to interactive brand experiences.

- **Voice Search Optimization**: With the rise of voice-activated devices like smart speakers, optimizing content for voice search will become a necessity.

The Mobile-First Approach

Mobile devices have become an inseparable part of consumers' lives. As such, a mobile-first approach will continue to be pivotal for marketers:

- **Mobile-Optimized Content**: Creating content that is easily consumable on mobile devices will be essential. This includes responsive design, faster loading times, and thumb-friendly interfaces.

- **Location-Based Marketing**: Utilizing GPS data for hyper-local targeting and personalized offers will become more sophisticated.

Privacy and Ethical Considerations

Consumer concerns about data privacy and ethical marketing practices will continue to shape the industry. Marketers must prioritize transparency and ethical behavior:

- **Data Privacy Compliance**: Stricter regulations around data privacy, such as GDPR and CCPA, will necessitate comprehensive compliance measures.

- **Ethical Data Usage**: Marketers should establish ethical data usage policies, respecting user consent and preferences.

Content Continues to Reign

Quality content remains the cornerstone of online marketing, and its importance will only increase:

- **Content Personalization**: AI-driven content personalization will be standard, delivering tailored experiences to each user.

- **Video Dominance**: Video content will continue to dominate, with short-form video formats gaining popularity on social media platforms.

Multi-Channel Integration

Consumers engage with brands across various touchpoints, and integrating marketing efforts across channels is vital:

- **Omnichannel Marketing**: Seamlessly connecting online and offline touchpoints will be essential for providing a unified customer experience.
- **Cross-Platform Advertising**: Coordinated advertising campaigns across platforms will ensure consistent brand messaging.

Sustainability and Social Responsibility

As consumers become more socially and environmentally conscious, brands will need to align with values and demonstrate social responsibility:

- **Green Marketing**: Brands should adopt sustainable practices and transparently communicate their eco-friendly initiatives.
- **Cause-Driven Marketing**: Supporting social causes and charitable efforts can resonate with socially conscious consumers.

Navigating an Evolving Search Landscape

Search engine algorithms are continually changing, affecting SEO strategies:

- **BERT and Natural Language Processing**: Understanding user intent and providing relevant content will be crucial in the wake of algorithm updates like BERT.
- **Structured Data Markup**: Implementing structured data to enhance search results and voice search compatibility will be standard.

The Globalization of Markets

The digital world transcends borders, opening opportunities for global expansion:

- **Localization and International SEO**: Adapting content for different languages and cultures will be essential for global reach.
- **Global Social Media Presence**: Building a strong social media presence across multiple countries and regions will require localized strategies.

Conclusion

Online marketing is a dynamic field, and the future promises both challenges and opportunities. Staying informed, flexible, and forward-thinking is paramount for success. By embracing technological advancements, prioritizing ethical practices, and remaining customer-centric, marketers can navigate the evolving landscape with confidence. Remember that adaptability and continuous learning will be the keys to unlocking the full potential of online marketing in the years to come.